GALLEY MAGIC

Gibsons: June 15th
I stood on the shore. To the North East the channel was a kaleidoscope of spin-
nakers — I closed my eyes and saw white billowing sails. It was this day in 1792 that
Captain George Vancouver passed this way . . .

Arthur McGinnis

Gibsons Marina

B.C.'s Marine Playground

PREFACE

. . . Capt. Vancouver had departed from Birch Bay three days earlier on a twelve day junket, crossing the mighty Fraser delta into Burrard Inlet and progressing up Howe Sound and the Sunshine Coast, through to Jervis Inlet, before returning to Birch Bay.

One year had transpired since the "DISCOVERY" and the "CHATHAM" had left England on an expedition to the west coast of America under the command of 34 year old Captain George Vancouver. The "DISCOVERY", a 99-foot sloop, with a crew of 100, and the "CHATHAM", a 54-foot brig with a crew of 56, returned to England in the fall of 1795. Vancouver's mission took four and a half years and carried him completely around the world. He returned a hero, the entire crew intact save for a carpenter who had been sent home in chains on a passing ship . . . but that's another story. During the first year of his expedition, having sailed half-way around the world, Vancouver stopped at the island paradises of New Zealand, Tahiti and Hawaii.

On April 17, 1792, the expedition made land on North America near Cape Mendocino, California. Through the spring, summer and fall of 1792 the expedition travelled up the Strait of Juan de Fuca into Puget Sound and the Gulf of Georgia, naming such prominent landmarks as Mount Baker and Mount Rainier. The names of Vancouver's officers and friends: Vashon, Whidbey, Howe, Jervis, Townsend, Atkinson and hundreds of others remain eternally fixed in our geography.

It was on June 24, 1792, that Captain Vancouver dined with Captains Valdez and Galiano of the Mexican ships "MEXICANA" and "SUTIL". Together they sailed for the now favourite anchorage of Desolation Sound for the summer. By late summer Vancouver became the first European to navigate and chart the intricate channels of this vast waterway that divides Vancouver Island from the mainland.

So, having sailed and charted the coast to Calvert Island, the "DISCOVERY" and the "CHATHAM" rendezvoused with their supply ship, "DAEDALUS" (recipe p. 63), at Nootka on the west coast of Vancouver Island. They sailed from there on October 17, 1792, to winter in Hawaii, returning in the spring of 1793 to chart the coast north of Vancouver Island to Alaska before returning, once again to Hawaii.

It was during the winter 'respite' that Captain Vancouver and King Kamehameha I became buddies. They should be credited with establishing the Maui Race: after leaving their winter paradise in March, 1794, the "Chatham" was an easy winner making the crossing to Nootka in 30 days, beating the "DISCOVERY" which took 52 days to do the course.

Hawaii wasn't so kind to other worldly navigators for it was here on his second voyage around the world that Captain Cook was done in by the natives. It was also in Hawaii that Captain Kendrick, of the American ship "Washington" out of Boston, was killed by a ball from a British ship saluting him.

One ship drives east and another drives west
With the self-same winds that blow,
'Tis the set of the sails and not the gales
Which tells us the way to go.

ELLA WHEELER WILCOX, Winds of Fate

Copyright 1987 by
Bocas de Carmelo Publishing
P.O. Box 1520, Gibsons, B.C.
Canada V0N 1V0

Canadian Catalogue in Publishing Data

McGinnis, Arthur   1929
Marina, Gibsons   1984

Galley Magic

ISBN 09692964–0–1

1. Cookery   2. Cookery International   3. Title

Printed in Canada

ACKNOWLEDGEMENTS

As Producer —

_____ My stars are you, the contributors.

_____ My superstars are:
 Diana Gruner, my Assistant
 Ruth McGinnis, my Wife

_____ Special acknowledgement to:
 Johann Shoepke, Acapulco Discovery
 Moira Clement, Photography

_____ Source material from:
 Canadian Egg Marketing Board, Minute Rice, Knox
 and Bacardi is acknowledged.

_____ Thanks also to Linda Henry, Diana Gray & Grace Maberg

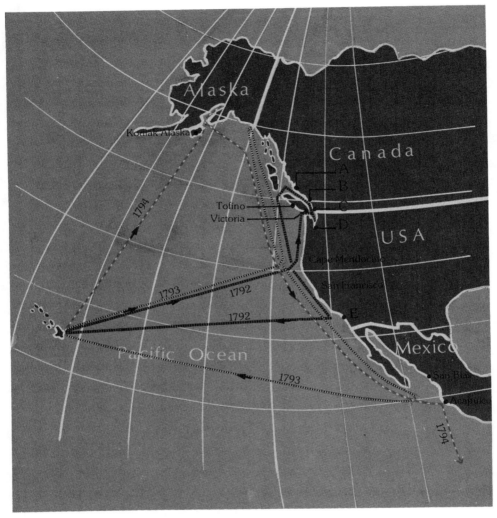

THE WESTERN SEABOARD OF NORTH AMERICA

The Travels of Capt. George Vancouver 1792-1794
"Voyage of Discovery" — Wintering in Hawaii.

A [Sullivan Bay
    Alert Bay
    Echo Bay]

B [Powell River
    Secret Cove
    Sechelt
    Gibsons
    Bocas de Carmelo]

C [Vancouver
    Birch Bay]

D [Orcas Island
    Everett
    Seattle]

E [Los Angeles
    New Port
    Balboa Bay
    Lodi]

CONTENTS

INTRODUCTION

In the beginning . . .

I must say it has been a very rewarding experience the past few years to meet so many of my old friends and make so many new ones. In addition to all our "permanent" boaters, the marina has been a temporary home port to thousands of visitors — always at their best when at play even after a particularly stormy and seemingly endless gulf crossing.

If there is a common thread that unites all boaters, it has to be cooking and coping in a galley — and so began this book — "Galley Magic". My original idea was simple — a compilation of boaters' favourite recipes — what could be easier than that? The more research I did, however, the more I realized that although much attention has been paid to the offshore sailor, the needs of the modern weekend boater seem to have been rather neglected.

"Galley Magic" was not intended to be a book of genius, showing you how to turn the simplest of ingredients into a gourmet's delight, or geared to intrigue and inspire the most jaded of cooks. The combined talents of all the contributors, however, has produced a book both useful and fun which we hope you will enjoy having on your boat or R.V.

Enjoy the book for where it can take you, an excursion through the gastronomic belt of the "western seaboard".

During the course of my research, I discover that since the first cookbook was published some 4,000 years ago, incredibly there is always a different ingredient or unique method that makes a recipe an "original". Many of the recipes in this book are our boaters' "originals" and for their contributions we thank them heartily.

Acknowledgement of sources of material in this book is not limited to prominent actors and politicians; stock and lumber brokers; doctors, lawyers and Stan Dixon; nor to the backs of cans and boxes. Thanks goes to all those chefs too numerous to mention who contributed (this is beginning to sound like the "Oscars").

Umberto Mengi once said, "I look for the author". Many of these "authors" are his patrons!!

Seriously, though, the idea of "Galley Magic" is to provide an on-hand reference book for working within the confines of the galley. Throughout the book are various tables and charts for quick on-board reference.

At this point I encourage you to be inventive and create your own variables — enjoy the magic!

Unlike many cookbooks, the recipes in "Galley Magic" have not always been tested — improvements have been left to you. So, CAST OFF!! Your recreation was Captain George Vancouver's vocation. For many your horizons will be Orcas, Keats or Merry Islands; Puget, Howe or Desolation Sounds. Some will experience inland waterways to the north coast and Alaska; for a few the Sea of Cortez or the Maui Race!!

But for ALL the sea! And Galley Magic!!

EQUIVALENTS

Abbreviations:

t	=	teaspoon	pt	=	pint
T	=	tablespoon (3t)	qt	=	quart
c	=	cup	oz	=	ounce
L	=	liter	lb	=	pound
g	=	gram	mL	=	milliliter
kg	=	kilogram			

Volume (Dry & Liquid)

$^1/_4$ t   =   1 mL
$^1/_2$ t   =   2 mL
1 t   =   5 mL
1 T (3 t)   =   15 mL
$^1/_4$ c   (4 T)   (2 oz)   =   50 mL
$^1/_3$ c   =   75 mL
$^1/_2$ c   (8 T)   (4 oz)   =   125 mL
1 c   (16 T)   (8 oz)   =   250 mL
2 c   (1 pt)   (16 oz)   =   500 mL
4 c   (1 qt)   (32 oz)   =   1000 mL

Utensils (More or Less)

Baking	—	8″ sq. × 2″	= 2 L
Loaf	—	9″ × 5″ × 3″	= 2 L
Casserole	—	2 qt	= 2 L +
Custard Cup	—	6 oz	= 200 mL

Weight

1 oz	=	30 g
4 oz ($^1/_4$ lb	=	115 g
8 oz ($^1/_2$ lb)	=	250 g
16 oz (1 lb	=	500 g
32 oz (2 lb)	=	1000 g

Temperature

275 F	=	140 C
300 F	=	150 C
325 F	=	160 C
350 F	=	180 C
375 F	=	190 C
400 F	=	200 C
425 F	=	220 C
450 F	=	230 C

ALWAYS USE LEVEL MEASURES

"The Voyage of Discovery"
   H.M. Ships "DISCOVERY" & "CHATHAM"

'Victualling Office
28th Dec. 1790

'Sir,
   'Having received orders to cause His Majesty's Armed Tender Chatham, under your command at Deptford, which is ordered to be fitted out at Woolwich for a voyage to remote parts — to be victualled to twelve months of all species of Provisions except Beer of which she is to have as much as she can conveniently stow, and supplied with Wine or Spirits in lieu of the remainder, for her complement mentioned on the other side, for Foreign Service: — We desire you will let us know the quantity of each species necessary for that purpose, and when she will be ready for the receiving thereof, in order to our sending the same on board: — and we beg you will be very particular in describing the sizes of the casks the Chatham can best stow.
                  'We are,
                   'Sir,
                     'Your most hum servts
                        'G. P. Lowry
                        'S. Marshall
                        'W. Boscawn
                        'Fred Stephens
'To the Commander Chatham armed tender Deptford.'

THE HANDLING OF FOODS

The handling of foods is often taken for granted in these days of refrigeration. Therefore I thought it was important to include a handy reference guide on basic methods for storing and preparing raw ingredients. I have been particularly explicit in the sections on fish and seafood as these foods are often dealt with live and proper storage is essential.

FISH

Fish is cooked to enhance its flavour rather than for tenderizing. Overcooking should be avoided as it toughens otherwise tender flesh. The magic of cooking fish is in timing. The following is a guide to cooking times for fish.

OVEN

Fresh or thawed * — 10 minutes per inch thickness
Partially thawed — 12-15 minutes per inch
Frozen (solid) — 20 minutes per inch

MICROWAVE

To thaw — 4-5 minutes per lb on defrost with equal standing time
Fresh or thawed — 4-5 minutes per pound

*Thaw in original wrapper in refrigerator or under cold running water for a quicker thaw.

It is recommended that fish not be cleaned if it is going to be filleted after catching. Some fish may be frozen completely intact (remove gills), particularly sockeye; however, coho, if not frozen immediately, should be cleaned due to its high level of cavity acid.

BOTTOM FISH (Ling cod, rock cod, snapper)

These fish are delectable and lend themselves to a wide variety of dishes. Being mild flavoured, one should avoid strong spices (mild herbs, dry white wine, are recommended).

The most common preparation of the meat of these fish is in fillet form. One way to fillet is to keep fish intact with head, tail and uncleaned cavity. Taking care not to puncture the cavity, make a cut vertically through the meat just behind the gills and fin. Then turn your knife parallel to the backbone and in a stroking motion "feeling the bone", cut along until you almost reach the tail. Stop before cutting through skin at tail. To remove skin from fillet, fold fillet over, laying skin down, and with knife flat to skin, cut fillet from skin in a sawing action. When barbequing, you may leave skin on and grill skin side down (oops! — now you tell me).

SALMON

Almost as above except in two cuts. Run your knife firstly flat along the belly, knife tip at a 45 degree angle as far as spine, starting at the tail end and working forward. Repeat on back side from tail forward, knife flat to bones in both cases. Then cut at gills — fold over to remove skin as above (if desired). Voila!!

It should be noted that salmon in general should be bled when caught. A common occurrence in cleaning salmon is the scraping out of the blood from the back of the body cavity — this should not be done as it breaks the cavity lining which helps to keep the fish fresh. Generally, uncooked fish will keep two days in the refrigerator. Cooked leftovers should be refrigerated and consumed "next day".

Bragging may not bring happiness, but no man having caught a large fish goes home through an alley.

ANONYMOUS

MOLLUSKS

Oysters, clams and mussels are generally at their best in seasons other than the summer when they are spawning, at which time their texture and flavour is not at peak.

pic/Heidi, page 17, (witness my daughter, Heidi. Picture on a damp July day in the Gulf Islands with empty oyster shells at her feet.)

Mollusks are the shellfish about which most concern over red tide should be had. Before collecting, look for postings or telephone your nearest Fisheries office.

OYSTERS

Oysters in the shell will stay alive in a cool moist place for weeks. Be sure to discard any with open shells. To open, attack an oyster with a blunt oyster knife with the deep half of the shell down (flat side up). Insert the knife near the hinge and pry open, severing the muscle connection to the top shell with a pivoting motion. Maintaining pressure against the shell, run the knife around the perimeter. Save the liquor to use as the cooking liquid or in which to store the oysters. Shucked oysters will keep a week refrigerated. Frozen oysters should be thawed in the refrigerator or in cold water — never at room temperature.

CLAMS & MUSSELS

A desirable step before cooking or opening clams is to place them in fresh cool seawater for a few hours to filter out sand (add rolled oats or cornmeal if available). Although eaten more often steamed, clams and mussels are opened fresh in much the same way as oysters. Discard any open shells before cooking. Once steamed, they open widely — discard any that do not.

CRAB

There is the way to cook crab where you throw it in a large pot of boiling seawater and then there is the way to do it within the confines of a galley.

Grasp the crab legs and claws from the rear close to the body to avoid being caught with the pincers. With shell up, rap the leading edge of the body shell on a protuding object to remove — then break the body in half lengthwise — clean in water — cook immediately in salted boiling water in halves. After cooking break between the legs to the centerline. Each crab makes 10 pieces — get it? Cool crab quickly by dunking it in cold water after cooking.

PRAWNS

Bjorn's Way — Fresh whole — in a suitably large pot lay in lots of dill, fresh or dried. Fill half way with prawns and cover with cold seawater adding 2 tablespoons of coarse salt. Place pot on high heat, allow to boil for one minute, then remove from heat and let stand until it cools enough to put your finger in the water comfortably — drain. Serve warm or cold with melted garlic butter and lots of white wine. Mmmm!

My Way (Bjorn's is better) — if your stove is slow to boil a large pot, bring your dilled, salted water to a boil and then add the prawns. When the water returns to a boil and top prawns float, remove pot from heat, drain and cool. With a slow stove turn the prawns over once to assure that bottom prawns do not overcook — time depends on how fast your stove is.

Peter's Way — in hot skillet sprinkled with salt saute whole prawns until slightly blackened. Turn and repeat on other side.

NOTES

— Thaw frozen prawns in cold water, not at room temperature.

— Heads-off prawns cook a little faster so be quick.

— If you wish to saute or bake prawns — peel fresh and butterfly — cut along the back partially through.

  — To peel cooked prawns — remove the head, peel off 2 shell segments, pinch the tail (where the meat is, silly — this is not *magic*) and out it pops.

For Seafood Sauces see page 25.

EGGS

— When beating egg whites add a little vinegar to improve foaming.
— Cover leftover yolks with water and refrigerate.
— Break eggs on a flat surface rather than a bowl's edge — reduces bits of shell falling into the egg.
— Do not leave egg dishes or those containing mayonnaise in the sun. Keep hot foods hot; cold foods cold.
— Devilled eggs won't wobble on the serving platter if you level them by slicing a small piece from the round bottom of each half.

Among the provisions Capt. Vancouver's expedition put on board were live sheep, pigs, chickens and the like. I imagine the question did arise about (the egg-ah-chicken) chicken. Could this be the origin of today's expression, "What comes first, the chicken or the egg?"

There is more on eggs in the Stovetop Section.

DAIRY PRODUCTS

MILK

Drink Your Milk!! — It's Great With Scotch!! (Remember to add milk to Scotch, not vice versa).

Milk should be stored at 39 degrees F or lower. If temperature should rise to, say, 50 degrees, storage life can be lowered to only 2 days instead of 10 (see chart). Leave milk in its original container.

CHEESE

For me, cheese is a wonderful mystery! Did you know:

— it takes a gallon of milk to make a pound of cheese?
— cheese is aged from 2-18 months?
— 4 oz. ungrated cheese equals 1 cup of grated?
— there are five cheese groups — soft, e.g. camembert; semi-soft, e.g. mozzarella; firm, e.g. cheddar; fresh, e.g. cottage cheese; hard, e.g. parmesan; and that these five groups produce hundreds of varieties of cheese?
— cheese should be stored closed in its original package for longer life?

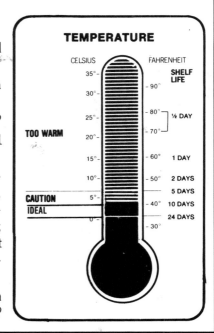

TEMPERATURE

CELSIUS	FAHRENHEIT	SHELF LIFE
35°	90°	
30°	80°	½ DAY
25°	70°	
TOO WARM 20°		
15°	60°	1 DAY
10°	50°	2 DAYS
		5 DAYS
CAUTION 5°	40°	10 DAYS
IDEAL 0°		24 DAYS
	30°	

16

MEATS

— Use refrigerated ground or variety meats within a day or two. Use refrigerated roasts within 3 or 4 days.

— Generally thaw frozen meats before cooking.

— Bring to room temperature before cooking by removing from refrigerator for approximately one hour.

— Best buys are always good cuts carefully aged.

— When cooking pork, use tender cuts and cook thoroughly.

— Organ meats, such as heart, liver, kidneys, etc., do not keep well and are a distant choice for on-board fare.

POULTRY

— Chicken is the most versatile of meats when it comes to choosing cooking technique.

— Chicken, either raw or cooked, should not be kept refrigerated over 2 days — either freeze or eat.

— Cooking raw chicken enables it to be kept refrigerated for a further two days.

— For on board convenience buy chicken breasts de-boned.

VEGETABLES

— Vegetables deserve the best efforts of every cook.

— Wash thoroughly — do not peel until ready to use.

— Use seasonings sparingly — they should enhance, not over-whelm.

— Use less than the freshest vegetables and leftovers in soups and casseroles.

INGREDIENTS OF NUTRITION

Although not stressing the nutritional side of "eating", a brief review of basics is worthy of some attention. There are four basic food groups which everyone should include in their daily diet.

Milk & Milk Products — Choose from fresh, skimmed, buttermilk, powdered milk, cheese, yogurt, cottage cheese and ice cream, many of which are served in soups, sauces, custards, etc.

Meat and Meat Alternatives — Foods of this group include meats, poultry, fish, eggs, nuts, dried beans and peas.

Breads and Cereals — These foods such as breads, grains, noodles, and spaghetti should be of the enriched or whole grain variety.

Fruits and Vegetables — Citrus fruits, tomatoes, apples, bananas, cauliflower, baked potatoes, carrots and leafy vegetables are all good sources of vitamins and fibre.

To all groups add a little oil for healthier skin and hair.

HANDY TIPS FOR IMPROVING YOUR NUTRITION

— Add wheat germ and bran to cakes, cookies, bread, meat loaf, etc., for extra B vitamins and fibre.

— Add skim milk powder to muffins, quick breads, etc., to neutralize baking soda/powder and add calcium.

— Use yogurt instead of sour cream in toppings, dips, etc. for fewer calories, less fat and yogurt's quality of aiding beneficial bacteria. Dress up with chives, spices, garlic, etc.

— Replace a meat meal with one of dried beans or peas at least once a week for lower fat, cholesterol and calories. Serve with grain or rice for complete protein.

They say regular eating of onions and garlic guards one against catching colds — maybe it's just that no one gets close enough to give you one??

INGREDIENT SUBSTITUTION

1 t baking powder	$^1/_4$ t baking soda + $^3/_4$ t cream of tartar
1 c granulated sugar	1 c brown sugar, firmly packed
1 T cornstarch (thickening)	2 T flour or 2 t quick cooking tapioca
1 c butter	1 c margarine (hard or brick) or 1 c shortening
1 c liquid honey	$1^1/_4$ c sugar + $^1/_4$ c liquid
1 c corn syrup	1 c sugar + $^1/_4$ c liquid
1 c buttermilk or sour milk	1 T lemon juice or vinegar + enough milk to make 1 c (let stand for 5 mins.)
1 c sour cream	1 c plain yogurt
1 c milk	$^1/_2$ c evaporated milk + $^1/_2$ c water
1 c skim milk	1 c water + 3 T skim milk powder
1 c cream	$^3/_4$ c milk + $^1/_4$ c butter
1 oz chocolate (1 square)	3 T cocoa + 1 T butter or shortening
1 whole egg	2 egg yolks
1 c tomato juice	$^1/_2$ c tomato sauce + $^1/_2$ c water
1 c tomato sauce	$^1/_2$ c tomato paste + $^1/_2$ c water
1 c tomato ketchup	1 c tomato sauce + $^1/_2$ c sugar + 2 T vinegar
1 clove garlic	$^1/_8$ t garlic powder
1 t dry mustard	1 T prepard mustard
1 small onion	1 T dehydrated, minced onion
1 T fresh herbs	1 t dried (parsley, oregano, etc.)
Juice of 1 lemon	3-4 T bottled lemon juice

GENERAL COOKING TERMS

Bake: To cook by dry heat (uncovered) in oven. Termed "roast" when applied to meat.

Baste: To moisten food while cooking with liquid or fat.

Beat: To incorporate air into a mixture by beater, spoon or mixer.

Blanch: To immerse foods briefly in boiling water, followed by a quick cooling in cold water.

Blend: To combine ingredients without excessive mixing.

Broil: To cook by direct heat under broiler or over coals.

Dredge: To coat completely with flour or sugar.

Fillet: A piece of meat, poultry or fish without bones.

Flake: To break food into small pieces, usually with fork.

Fold: To combine one ingredient with another very gently to avoid loss of air.

Grate: To rub a food against a grater to form small particles.

Julienne: To cut meat or vegetables into long matchlike strips.

Marinate: To let food stand in a seasoned sauce called a marinade to tenderize and increase flavour.

Parboil: To partially cook food in a boiling liquid. Cooking is usually completed by another method.

Poach: To cook food over low heat in simmering liquid.

Saute: To brown or cook in a skillet in a small amount of fat.

Scald: To heat liquid to just below boiling point, to pour boiling water over food or dip in boiling water.

Sear: To brown the surface of foods quickly.

Season: To add salt and pepper, also the term used for preparing cooking equipment or bakeware.

Simmer: To cook in liquid just below the boiling point.

Skim: To remove fat or film from surface of food.

Steam: To cook over, not in, boiling water.

Stew: To simmer slowly in liquid deep enough to cover.

Stir: To mix ingredients in a circular motion until blended with uniform consistency.

Stir-fry: To cook in frypan or wok over high heat in a small amount of fat, tossing or stirring constantly.

Toast: To brown with dry heat in an oven or toaster.

Toss: To tumble ingredients lightly with lifting motion.

Whip: To beat rapidly with wire whisk, beater or mixer to incorporate air and increase volume.

WINES & SPIRITS

Wine has often been described as the *magic* ingredient in cooking. It can impart new zest and flavour to transform a humdrum dish into a festive offering.

Use wine as you would other seasonings. Its use in place of water adds an elusive flavour. Wine itself is not detectible when it blends with food flavours so if you taste wine in your cooking you've used too much — just as in spicing, wine should not dominate a dish.

If you ask what wine you should use in cooking — simply use some of the wine you have selected as a beverage with your dinner. Purloin what you need for cooking or basting in your galley from the same bottle you are serving at the table.

There are no rules in what wine to use and whether it should be red or white so your choice should be guided only by the general custom of red wines with dark ingredients (red meats) and white with light (poultry, seafoods). Wine should only be heated, not boiled. For example, add wine to your soup after removing it from the stove. Wines should also be dry rather than sweet.

Beer can also produce some very interesting and satisfying results. Just remember the fundamental rule of less is better than more in all cooking with alcohol.

Brandy, of course, has always been a favourite ingredient of adventuresome cooks. However, it is important when flambeing brandy to not only set the liquor aflame but to reduce the quantity somewhat by evaporation to remove the raw taste of alcohol. When using distilled spirits in cooking — again — use discretion. A splash of tequila, whiskey or rum can transform today's dish as well as tomorrow's leftover. Proceed with confidence!!

Cooking is like love. It should be entered into with abandon or not at all.

HARRIET VAN HORNE

SPICES WITH HERBS & SEEDS

The lure of eastern spices set Columbus on his way long after Marco Polo had blazed spice trails across Asia as far away as Cathay. The routes of conquest of Darius the Persian and Alexander the Great also cut through the sub-tropical spice band from the shores of Africa to Indonesia. However, the Orient is no longer the "Far East" and today we have easy access to specialties from around the world.

In the distant past spirits were used in preserving, adding pleasant flavours to salted or aging meats. New methods of preserving, however, together with advances in refrigeration, have changed spicing from a "necessity" to the enjoyable addition to our foods of an infinite variety of flavours.

The following chart is comprehensive as a reference guide — in it "spice" has been used to also include herbs and seeds.

Recipes here have been screened to protect you from being "burned"!! Szechuan, chili and other "hot" dishes which require a "miracle of recovery" of your taste buds have been left to specialty cuisine — green and serano chilies (remove seeds — they are hot!!) have been included in some recipes — however, on a hotness scale of 100 these only rate a 10 or 15 and enhance rather than hide flavours.

Spicing doubles the pleasure of food — it gives the mind something to feed upon while the appetite is being satisfied; indeed, the pleasure is tripled for the chef!!

NOTES

— Recipes are based on dried herbs (unless otherwise noted). Use three times as much fresh herbs as dried.

   — Keep spices in closed containers in a cool, dry place.

   — Spices should enhance not overpower the flavour of food so use less rather than more to start.

   — Add spices in the latter part of cooking — overheating can cause spices to turn bitter.

ART'S HERB & SPICE REVERSE CHART

(More Things go with Most Things than not!!)

Spice	Flavour	Not Recommended With	Not Big With
* Allspice	Sweet, mild, spicy	Vegies, seafood	Beef, poultry
* Anise	Sweet, licorice	Seafood	Meats, vegies
Basil	Delicate, sweet	Bread, cakes, desserts	Meats
* Bay leaves	Mild, sweet	Bread, cakes, desserts	Eggs
* Caraway	Sharp, sweet	Poultry, seafood	Meats
* Cardamom	Bittersweet	Meats, poultry, seafood	Eggs
Cayenne	Hot	Breads, cakes, desserts	
* Celery seed	Tangy, aromatic	Breads, desserts	
* Chervil	Mild, aromatic	Breads, cakes, desserts	Meats
Chili powder	Fierce, distinctive	Breads, cakes, desserts	Vegies
* Cinnamon	Sweet, spicy	Meats, poultry, seafood	Vegies, Eggs
* Cloves	Sweet, spicy, pungent	Seafood, poultry	Vegies
* Cilantro	Sharp, clean	Meats, cakes, desserts	
Coriander	Sweet, pungent	Seafoods, desserts	
* Cumin	Pungent, warm	Seafoods	
Curry	Aromatic, hot, spicy	Breads, cakes, desserts	
Dill	Mild, sharp	Poultry	Meats
* Fennel	Anise-like	Seafood, poultry	Vegies
* Fenugreek	Bitter, pleasant	Breads, cakes, desserts	
* Ginger	Sweet, sharp		Vegies
* Mace	Sweet, warm	Poultry, seafoods	Vegies
Marjoram	Delicate, spicy	Breads, cakes, desserts	
* Mint	Sweet, cool	Poultry, beef	Seafood
Mustard	Sharp, spicy	Cakes, desserts	Breads
* Nutmeg	Like mace	Poultry	Meats
Oregano	Pungent, strong	Bread, cakes, desserts	
* Paprika	Mild, sweet, hot	Bread, cakes, desserts	
Parsley	Mild, pleasant	Bread, cakes, desserts	
Pepper	Spicy, enduring	Bread, cakes, desserts	
* Rosemary	Bittersweet	Bread, cakes, desserts	Seafood
* Saffron	Warmly bitter	Meats, vegies	
* Sage	Bitter, pungent	Breads, cakes, desserts	Vegies
Savory	Piquant, mild	Breads, cakes, desserts	Seafood
Sesame seed	Nutty	Eggs	
Tarragon	Tart, astringent	Bread, cakes, desserts	Meat, fruits
Thyme	Pleasant, distinctive	Bread, cakes, desserts	Vegies
Turmeric	Mild, pungent	Vegies, cakes, desserts	Eggs

FOR WHAT A SPICE OR HERB IS REALLY GOOD FOR, READ LABEL

* Starred items not suggested for basic on board.

Curry is composed of:- Cumin, fenugreek, turmeric, chili, corian-der, cinnamon, nutmeg and mace.

The Chinese "5" spices are:- Anise, fenugreek, ginger, cinnamon and pepper.

S
A
U
C
E
S

It is quite likely that the course of history could have been changed by sauces. Not long after George returned home to Britain, the "Great Mutiny" of April 1797 took place which completely shut down the British Navy. Food was a principal cause. In those dark days, "Britain did not rule the waves".

The presentation here of a broad spectrum of sauces has been provided to avoid the possibility of mutiny on your weekend outing. Such a revolt can be averted, however. Sauces can add inspiration to your cooking; make average foods incredible; add a special flavour to vegetables; and give a zest to leftovers.

As chef of the "Tesilya", and in preparation for the month long circumnavigation of Vancouver Island in "Islands Odyssey '86", Mary Waller had among the stores a variety of packaged sauce mixes. As Mary says:

"I particularly liked Knorr's Hunter, Green Pepper and Curry and Mayacama's Marinara, Pesto and Alfredo sauces. This was my first experience cooking on a boat and, not knowing when we would be able to get fresh food, I relied heavily on sauces . . ."

SAUCY TIPS

— Use stainless steel or ceramic pots for sauces with wines, acids, or acidic foods (tomatoes, lemons, etc.).

— For a quick compatible sauce to a browned food add vinegar, wine or water to the pan. Stir, add herbs and cream and simmer lightly.

— The use of unsalted butter allows more recognition of herbal or spice flavours.

— Reduction sauces are ideal for maintaining flavour. Reducing liquids by slow simmering thickens sauces without starch. (nouvelle cuisine).

— If you want to prepare a sauce for a recipe ahead of time, take a tablespoon of butter and break it into small pieces. Dot it on the surface of the sauce and gently spread around with a fork. This will prevent a skin from forming.

— Lay your prepared foods on the sauce rather than pouring the sauce over (for example, pollo mole on page 41).

— Use a wire whisk to blend your sauces.

— Always add mustard near end of cooking — don't boil as it will impart a bitter flavour.

See Bbq section for marinades and bbq sauces. Other sauces are included with specific recipes throughout the book.

BASIC WHITE SAUCE

2 T	butter or marg.	Melt butter and slowly stir in flour.
2 T	flour	Cook 5 mins. stirring constantly. Remove from heat.
2 c	hot milk	Stir in 1/2 c milk till smooth, return
1/2	onion (in one piece)	pan to stove on low heat, slowly stir in remaining milk. Add onion, simmer on low 30 mins., uncovered, stirring occasionally. Remove onion and serve.

HOT BUTTER SAUCES

Melted butter or margarine, flavoured with herbs and seasonings, is perfect with cooked fish or shellfish. Simply melt and stir in remaining ingredients to taste. All spices and other ingredients should be finely chopped or shredded. Each recipe makes about 1/2 cup.

LEMON-GARLIC-BUTTER SAUCE

1/2 c	butter/marg.
1 clove	garlic
1 t	lemon peel
2 T	lemon juice
1/2 t	chives/gr. onion tops

LIME-BUTTER SAUCE

1/2 c	butter/marg.
1 t	lime peel
1 T	lime juice
1-2 t	cilantro/parsley

DILL-BUTTER SAUCE

1/2 c	butter/marg.
2-3 t	lemon juice
2-3 t	fresh dill or
1 t	dry dill weed

NUT-BUTTER SAUCE

1/2 c	butter/marg.
2 T	almonds/peanuts/ pinenuts, chopped

Melt butter, add nuts, heat till lightly toasted.

LIME-GINGER-BUTTER SAUCE

6 T	butter/marg.
1 T	fresh lime juice
2 t	gingerroot, grated

MUSTARD-CAPER-BUTTER SAUCE

1/2 c	butter/marg.
1 t	dry mustard
1 T	lemon juice
1/2 t	capers
1 T	parsley

ANCHOVY BUTTER SAUCE

1/2 c	butter/marg.
3	anchovies, rinsed dried and mashed
1 clove	garlic
1/4 t	lemon juice

TARRAGON-BUTTER SAUCE

1/2 c	butter/marg.
1 T	lemon juice
1 1/2 t	tarragon

BASIL BUTTER SAUCE

1/2 c	butter/marg.
4 t	basil, dried or
1/4 c	fresh basil
2 t	lemon juice

HONEY MUSTARD SAUCE

1/2 c	butter/marg.
2 T	honey
1 T	dijon mustard or
2 t	dry mustard

THE CLASSICS

BERNAISE   For steak, fish and eggs

3	gr. onions, chopped	Combine and simmer till reduced
$1/2$ c	vinegar	to 2 T. Strain and cool.
1 t	tarragon	
2	egg yolks	Beat slightly and blend in.
2 T	cream	Add cream then over low heat,
$1/2$ c	butter (unsalted)	stirring constantly, add cold
to taste	salt and pepper	butter little by little until
		thickened. Do not boil.

CHORON   For steak, chicken and fish

3	gr. onions, chopped	Combine and simmer till reduced
$1/4$ c	white wine vinegar	to 2 T. Strain and cool.
$1/4$ c	dry white wine	
2	egg yolks	Beat slightly and blend in.
$1/2$ c	butter (unsalted)	Add half of cold butter in
		block, stirring till melted.
		Then add other half till
		thickened.
2 T	tomato paste	Stir in.

BEURRE BLANC   For fish

1 T	gr. onion, chopped	Combine and simmer till reduced
2 T	white wine vinegar	to 1 T.
2 T	dry white wine	
1 c	butter	Whisk in little by little till
to taste	salt and pepper	creamy.

Variation: Replace wine with 1 T sherry.

HOLLANDAISE

For vegies and eggs

¹/₂ c	butter	Mash, soften in stainless steel bowl over pan of hot water.
3	egg yolks	Beat in one by one till creamy.
1 T	lemon juice	Add and cook, stirring till
pinch	salt	thickened. Do not boil.
¹/₄ c	boiling water	Add slowly, stirring till
2 T	tequila or sherry	thickened.

If sauce curdles, quickly beat in a few drops of cold water and another egg yolk.

Variation:

1 T	orange peel and/	Add to hollandaise.
1 T	or orange juice	

MOUSSELINE

For seafood

3 parts	hollandaise, cooled	Blend together. Serve
1 part	stiff whipped cream	immediately.

VELOUTE

For fish

1¹/₂ T	butter or margarine	Melt butter over low heat.
1¹/₂ T	flour	Stir in flour, cook over low heat 4 mins.
1 c	clam juice salt and pepper	Stir in gradually. Cook till thickened.

SUPREME

For eggs, fish, poultry, vegies

1 c	veloute sauce	See recipe above.
2	egg yolks	Blend together and add to
2 T	heavy cream	veloute.
2 T	butter	Cube and stir in gradually.

DESSERT SAUCES

CHOCOLATE SAUCE

2 oz	chocolate, unsweetened	Break up chocolate, add water. Cook over low heat till
10 T	water	smooth. Do not boil.
2 t	cornstarch	Combine and stir into
3 T	water	chocolate.
4 T	butter	Add and cook for a few mins.
6 T	sugar	
to taste	vanilla extract	Add after removal from heat.

RUM SAUCE

6	egg yolks	Beat egg yolks slightly. Add
8 T	butter	remaining ingredients stirring
$1/2$ c	thick cream	over low heat till thickened.
$1/2$ c ea.	sugar and rum	
1 t	cornstarch	

RAISIN SAUCE   Also for ham and pork

$1^1/2$ c	water	Combine and boil for 15 mins.
$1/3$ c	seeded raisins	
$1/4$ c	sugar	
$1/8$ t	salt	
2 T	butter, melted	Mix. Slowly add some hot sauce,
1 t	flour	return to pan, stir and cook till boiling and thickened.
to taste	nutmeg/lemon rind	Mix in.

HOT AND SPICY

SPICY PEANUT SAUCE
For chicken or lamb

$^1/_4$ c	gr. onions, chopped	Saute in small amount of oil
1 clove	garlic	till golden.
1 cube	chicken bouillion	Mix and add to onions.
1 c	boiling water	
$^1/_4$ c	peanuts	Grind in blender and add.
1 T	soya sauce	Add to above. Bring to boil.
1 t	brown sugar	stirring constantly. Simmer
$^1/_2$ t	lime juice	10 mins.
$^1/_8$ t ea.	coriander and ginger	
1	dry chili, crumbled	

WALNUT SAUCE
For beef or chicken

$^1/_2$ c	plain yogurt	Mix together.
2 T	walnuts, pounded	
1 T	horseradish	

PEPPER SAUCE
For lamb, steak and hamburger

1 T	butter	Saute 4 mins.
2 T	gr. onions, chopped	
1 T	tequila/brandy	Add to onions and flame.
$^1/_4$ c	mayonnaise	Stir in and bring to boil.
1 T	dijon mustard	Simmer, stirring constantly,
1 T	white wine	till of desired consistency.
$^1/_2$ T	black peppercorns, lightly crushed or	
$^1/_4$ t	black pepper	

Doorman — La Hacienda. Restaurant — "Acapulco Princess."

In the fall of '86, Ruth and I attended a "Classe de Gastronomia Mexicana" at the Acapulco Princess.

During the fun filled week, Executive Chef Johann G. Schoepke guided his senior chefs of the Princess's seven restaurants in introducing us to a Mexican cuisine we didn't know existed. Exotic Mexican foods included carefully balanced ingredients, herbs and spices. I wanted to bring some of this Mexican magic to you and invited Johann to share a few pages on different and interesting ways to please your palate.

In the fall of 1794 HMS "Discovery" set anchor in Acapulco Harbour, the last leg on the journey home.

It was in the spring of 1791 that Capt. Vancouver, in his first command at 34 years of age, was entrusted with the sole direction of the expedition to the western seaboard of "North America".

ACAPULCO DISCOVERY

Vancouver's mission, as Commissioner, was to meet with the Spanish Captain Bodega y Quadra to settle claims arising out of the Nootka affair, the seizure by the Spaniards of British vessels in 1789. The two captains did not really understand the parameters of their directives since the vessels in question were long gone so they named Vancouver and Quadra Islands after themselves and departed friends. Vancouver's relationship with the Spanish out of Mexico was excellent so when he dropped in at Acapulco in the fall of '74 he received a warm welcome (margaritas and mariachi bands?).

Modern tastes are turning south to Mexico, a growing trend towards a spicy new experience in foods. Basic ingredients include the many varieties of chilies and peppers; herbs; tortillas and refried beans together with sauces in combination with cheeses and green peppers.

Many of the ingredients in the following recipes need no explanation but comment is made of a few of those that may be unfamiliar. The chili or pepper, a basic ingredient of Mexican cooking, should be treated with caution for although appealing when cooked in a recipe, it is to be respected in its handling. With some chilies it is even recommended that you wear gloves to prevent damage to sensitive skin!!

With ALL avoid eye contact (rubbing your eyes after peeling or chopping the chilies). To prepare chilies or peppers for cooking, quarter them, remove and dispose of the seeds and veins (they are wild!), finely cut lengthwise and cross chop. Serrano peppers are available in coastal stores from time to time. Fresh produce better results than cans — stock up when they are available in the stores and freeze them for later use.

Other ingredients worthy of a passing comment are:

Tortillas — thin pancakes made of corn or wheat flour, usually available on the coast in the frozen food department of supermarkets.

Cilantro — also known as Chinese parsley and available in most produce departments. It is a delightful (medium) herb and is accepted, chopped, in many dishes. Its seed is called coriander.

In Johann's recipes, where chili is called for it is to be seeded, veined then finely chopped.

Tomatoes are often treated specially by removing the seeds and therefore the bitterness. Cut in half and squeeze the juices and seeds out — only the pulp is then used.

CEVICHE ACAPULCO — *SALAD*   SERVES 6-10

1 lb	red snapper, not frozen	Cut fish into cubes, toss with lemon juice in ceramic or pyrex bowl. Cover with plate, keep in cool, dark place (not refrigerator) 6-8 hrs. Stir occasionally till cubes appear opaque. Squeeze gently as you pour off juice, set aside.
1/2 c	lemon juice	

4 T	olive oil	For the sauce — saute garlic gently.
4 cloves	garlic, chopped	

3	tomatoes, seeded, diced	Mix with garlic in large bowl. Season to taste with salt. Garnish with avocado chunks and serve chilled with salted crackers on the side.
2	onions, chopped	
3 oz	cilantro, chopped	
1	serrano chili	
20-30	gr. olives, whole	
1/4 t	oregano	
1 t	Worcester sauce	
2 T	ketchup	
6 T	tomato juice	
1/2 oz can	chili chipotle, chopped	

SINCRONIZADAS — *HOT APPETIZER*   SERVES 6

6 oz	fried beans	Spread beans equally over tortillas.
11 — 6″	tortillas	

6 slices	ham, cooked	Place on six of the tortillas.
12 slices	Velveeta cheese	

1 lg	onion, sliced fine	Cover ham and cheese with onion slices and sprinkle with chopped chilies, cover with remaining tortillas.
2	serrano chilies	

Hold tortillas together with 4 toothpicks each and cut into quarters, fry in very little oil, serve warm with guacamole sauce.

QUESADILLAS WITH SEA BASS - *STOVE-TOP* SERVES *6-8*

1¹/₂ lb	white fish fillets	Gently simmer fillets in a minimum of
1	carrot, chopped	water together with other ingredients
1 stalk	celery, chopped	until fish flakes easily with fork. Cool.
2	bay leaves	
3 lge	onions, cut in fine strips	Saute in a little oil for 3 mins. Reduce
2 cloves	garlic, finely chopped	heat, add fish and simmer 8 mins.
2 lge	tomatoes, seeded, diced	
	juice of 1 lemon	Add to above, mix well and simmer
2 oz	cilantro, fresh	2 mins. Cool.
1	serrano chili	
24	corn tortillas	Fill one half of each tortilla with filling, fold over other half, secure with tooth pick. At serving time, heat oil in skillet, lay in quesadillas, not too tightly, fry till crisp and golden. Dry on paper towel, serve on shredded lettuce with guacamole and Mexican sauce.

PICO DE GALLO — *SAUCE*

2 T	lemon juice	Assemble and use as a sauce.
4 T	orange juice	
1 sm	onion, chopped	
1 sm	serano chili, chopped	
1 bunch	cilantro, chopped	
	pineapple chunks	Pour sauce over vegetables.
	cucumber, chopped	
	carrots, sliced	
	gicamas, sliced	

RED SNAPPER PUERTO MARQUES - oven   SERVES 6-8

5 lb	red snapper, whole, cleaned	Pierce fish on both sides with sharp
3 T	lime juice	fork. Rub in juice and salt. Place in
2 T	salt	lightly oiled pan.

5 T	olive oil	Sauce:
2 lge	onions	Heat olive oil, add onion, carrots,
3	carrots	peppers and tomatoes, fry gently
1 each	bellpeppers, red, green, yellow	until onions are limp. Add mushrooms and garlic and fry for 5
3 lbs	tomatoes, unseeded	mins. more. Add olives, tomato
5 ozs	mushrooms	juice, water and salt and pepper to
8 cloves	garlic, whole	taste. Cook 8 mins. more.
10	green olives	
5 T	tomato juice	
1 c	water	
	salt and pepper	

Pour sauce over fish, cover pan and bake for 25 mins. at 375 degrees. Turn fish over and continue baking without cover 15 mins. more, basting with sauce every 5 mins. Garnish with fresh chopped cilantro and chili gueros — serve with potatoes or white rice and lemon wedges.

RED SNAPPER MEXICANA — oven   SERVES 4

$1^1/_2$ lb	red snapper fillets flour	Season fillets with salt and pepper, dip in flour and place in oiled baking dish.

2 lge	onions	Slice and lay over fillets.
2 lge	tomatoes	

2	serrano peppers	Sprinkle over top, bake at 375
4	bay leaves	degrees till fish flakes easily with a
$^1/_2$ t	oregano	fork.
$^1/_4$ c	cilantro, chopped	

CHALUPAS CAMPESINAS — COLD APPETIZER   SERVES 6-8

24	chalupas, 3″ diameter	These are very thin fried shells of tortilla dough. They are available in the supermarket.
10 oz 1	Spanish sausage, diced potato, boiled and diced	Fry sausage in own fat, add potatoes and cool.
10 oz	fried beans guacamole cheese, grated	Spread some beans on chalupas, cover with sausage mix and guacamole, sprinkle grated cheese on top. Serve cold. All items may be prepared ahead but assemble at last minute so chalupas will be crisp.

COLD MELON SOUP — SOUP   SERVES 4

3 $^1/_2$ pt $^1/_2$ pt 6 T	canteloupe lemon sherbert orange sherbert lemon juice	Cut melons in half, remove seeds. Scoop out half of two of the melons leaving a ring of pulp intact. Put in blender together with all of third melon, sherbert and lemon juice. Blend at high speed 30 secs. Strain.
6 oz to taste	port wine salt	Add wine and stir. Salt to taste.
	prosciutto ham, julienned	Fill reserved melon halves with soup and sprinkle ham over top. Serve very cold.

The first of all considerations is that our meals shall be fun as well as fuel.

ANDRE SIMON

POLLO MOLE — *MAIN DISH*

SERVES 4

4	**chicken breasts**	Split, skin, debone and place in glass or ceramic bowl.
$1/4$ c	**olive oil**	Combine and pour over chicken.
2 T	**lemon juice**	Marinate for 4 hrs., turning
1	**serrano pepper**	occasionally. Grill 4 mins. each side
1 clove	**garlic**	or till cooked through.
$1/4$ t	**cumin**	
4	**tortillas**	Arrange on plate, coat with mole sauce (below), place chicken on top. Serve guacamole sauce on the side.

MOLE SAUCE

6	**ancho chilies**	Soak chilies in hot water 30 mins.,
2 med	**onions**	drain, puree with other ingredients.
4 cloves	**garlic, chopped**	
1	**tortilla, slivered**	
3	**tomatoes, seeded**	
$1/2$ c ea.	**pine nuts, almonds and raisins**	
2 T	**sesame seeds**	
1 T	**cilantro, finely chopped**	
1 t ea.	**cumin seeds and ground coriander**	
$1/2$ t ea.	**anise and cinnamon**	
$1/4$ c	**vegetable oil**	Heat oil in large skillet, add puree,
2 c	**chicken stock**	cook over medium heat 5 mins.
$1^1/2$ oz	**unsweetened chocolate**	stirring constantly. Add stock,
to taste	**salt and pepper**	chocolate, salt and pepper. Stir till chocolate has melted then simmer uncovered 15 mins. or till flavours are combined.

41

A
P
P
E
T
I
Z
E
R
S

What could be said for hors d'oeuvres that hasn't already been said? — skewer it! toothpick it! finger it! For boaters, a standing start to the main course or will it be the main course??

It is often difficult to have guests "for dinner" on board — one way to deal with this is to have a "cocktail buffet".

Appetizer recipes can be expanded and more dishes can be offered — all selected to be handled with two fingers or a toothpick. Even though "hors d'oeuvres" literally translates into "out of the main course", you can combine hot and cold appetizers into a fun dinner party.

There has been a temptation to "star" recipes for appetizers and, indeed, for the entire book, but judgements are an individual experience for all of our senses — so you be the judge!!

SALMON SEVICHE

SERVES 4

Traditionally, whitefish and scallops are basics in seviche — this salmon approach is mouth watering. Large farm raised trout is also excellent prepared this way.

1 lb	salmon fillet	Slice salmon lengthwise $1/4''$ thick,
2 T	lime juice	marinate 1 hr. in lime and finely
1 T	serrano chili	chopped chilis (seeds removed!).
		Turn, add more lime juice, marinate
		1 hr. longer.

4 T	olive oil	Drain lime juice from salmon, blend
1	gr. onion, chopped	with oil, onion and spice. Arrange
1 T	ground corriander	salmon on serving dish and spoon
		sauce over, chill.

Oddvin Vedo, "TRESFJORD I", Sechelt, B.C.

SMOKED SALMON TAZA

SERVES 4

1 lb	smoked salmon	Using $1/2$ of salmon, uniformly line
		muffin tins or 4 oz foil or paper cups
		with finely sliced salmon, trim.

2 c	cream	Chop remaining salmon, combine
$1/2$ c	lemon juice	with other ingredients adding salt
$1/8$ c	fresh basil or parsley,	and pepper to taste. Stir till mixture
	chopped	thickens.

Pack in cups — refrigerate at least 4 hrs. Serve by running knife around edge and prying out of cups, arrange on platter.

2 T	ketchup	Blend, spoon over salmon and
$1/4$ c	white wine	serve.
$1/8$ t	dill weed	

Liz Leitner, "MY LIZ", Sechelt, B.C.

OYSTERS MAPLE SUGAR II

SERVES **4**

12	oysters in shell	Grill oysters. When opened $1/2''$
24 pcs.	cheddar cheese	insert a piece of cheese into each, grill till cheese melts.

Eat hot (with oven mitts) accompanied by white wine.

Kathy Harvey, "MAPLE SUGAR II", N. Vancouver, B.C.

CRAB KALAKUA

SERVES **4**

2	papaya, ripe	Halve and remove seeds.
2 T	butter	Saute garlic in butter, add flour,
1 sm		blend in cream, wine and pimiento,
clove	garlic	then add crab meat and spread into
3 T	flour	papaya. Place on rack in pan of
1 c	light cream	water.
1 T	dry vermouth	
1 T	pimiento	
$1/2$ lb	crabmeat	
2 T	parmesan cheese, grated	Sprinkle on papaya, bake at 350 degrees till heated and golden.

Marion Brant, "FOUR WINDS", Sechelt, B.C.

WINDSONG CLAMS

SERVES **4**

12/24	butter clams	Clean (p. 14), split with sharp knife.
2	eggs	Beat and dip each open side into
1 T	water	egg.
$1/4$ c	cornmeal	Dip in dry ingredients, fry meat side
2 T	flour	down till brown.
pinch	basil and cayenne	

Jim O'Donnell, "WINDSONG BARGE", Echo Bay, B.C.

SALMON & CREAM CHEESE BALL

1/2 lb	cream cheese	Cream together thoroughly.
2 T	mayonnaise	

1 1/2 lb	fresh cooked salmon or 1 lb canned	Mix together with above and shape into a ball.
1 T	horseradish	
1T	liquid smoke	
1 T	lemon juice	
1 T	dried parsley flakes	

Serve as an hors d'oeuvre or as first course at a dinner party. i.e., pate.

Meryn Rosback, "GYPSY V", Alert Bay, B.C.

EASY CHEESE BALLS

8 oz	Imperial Sharp Cheese/ cold pack	Blend at room teamperature and shape into a ball.
8 oz	Philadelphia cream cheese	
2 T	crisp bacon bits	
2 T	gr. onions, finely chopped	
1 T	Worcester sauce	
1 T	horseradish	
4 drops	tabasco sauce	

Roll cheese ball in mixture of chopped walnuts, pecans and/or parsley to cover. Easy To Make — Easy To Take!!

Dot Gibson, "MALIS", Tofino, B.C.

TINY SOYA DRUMSTICKS

3 lb	tiny drumsticks or chicken wings	Cut off drumstick ends (if using wings) and arrange in 13″ × 9″ × 2″ pan.
$^1/_4$ c	water	Mix together and pour over chicken.
$^1/_4$ c	dry sherry	Marinate for 3-4 hrs. in refrigerator.
$^1/_4$ c	dark soya sauce	Pour off liquid before baking.
$^1/_4$ c	honey	

Bake for 1 hr. at 350 degrees, baste every 20 mins. Serve with rice for main dish or sprinkle with sesame seeds as appetizer.

Heidi Lambert, "GIBSONS MARINA", Gibsons, B.C.

SWEDISH MEATETIZERS

1 lb	ground beef	Set aside $^1/_2$ c of the cream.
1$^1/_2$ c	bread crumbs	Combine rest of ingredients and
$^1/_2$ c	dry sherry	shape into 40-60 miniature meat
1$^1/_4$ c	heavy cream	balls.
$^1/_2$ t ea.	ground mace and salt	
$^1/_8$ t	pepper	
	flour	Coat meat balls in flour and brown well, drain on paper towels, set aside.
2 T	salad oil	Heat in cleaned skillet, stir in 1 T
2 T	butter	flour.
10 oz	beef consomme	Add gradually with the $^1/_2$ c cream, heat to boiling, stirring constantly.
1	bay leaf	Add, reduce heat, add meatballs, simmer 10-15 mins. covered.

Arlene McGinnis, "ANNIE", Tofino, B.C.

BANNER I ARTICHOKES

4	artichokes	Cook 14-15 mins. on high, cool and remove leaves.
	mayonnaise freshly cooked shrimp or prawn pieces	Place a small scoop of mayonnaise at the base of each leaf and top with several shrimp. Arrange decoratively on serving plate.

Helen Patterson, "BANNER I", Vancouver, B.C.

CHEESE SABLES

24 TRIANGLES

$^1/_4$ c $^1/_2$ c	butter flour, sifted	Cut together with pastry blender.
$^1/_2$ c to taste	aged cheddar cheese salt and pepper	Mix in and press into ball, chill 1 hr.
1	egg, beaten	Roll ball to $^1/_8$" thick on back of cookie sheet, brush with egg, cut into 2" strips, then cross-cut to form triangles.

Bake at 375 degrees for 10 mins. or till golden brown. Serve warm or store in air tight container.

Lisa Hanson, "DELIVERANCE", Corona del Mar, Ca.

HOT ARTICHOKE SPREAD

SERVES 4

14 oz can 1 c 1 c $^1/_2$ t	artichoke hearts, drained and chopped mayonnaise parmesan, grated garlic powder	Combine and mix well in glass pie plate, bake at 450 degrees for 20 mins. or till brown. Serve with crackers.

Mary Weberg, "THIS'L'DO", Skookumchuck Narrows, B.C.

PRAWNS LAURA COVE

3 cups	fresh prawns	Cook in boiling water, peel and cool.

2 T	peanut or olive oil	Heat oil in wok or frying pan 20 secs.
4 cloves	garlic, finely chopped	Add garlic and ginger, stir 15 secs.
6 T	black bean sauce	Add pepper, soya and cooked
2 t	ginger	prawns, stir fry 2-3 mins. Add black
dash	pepper and soya sauce	bean sauce, mix till well coated — they're done!

Enjoy as a "Happy Hour" hors d'oeuvre or on rice as part of dinner.

Brigid Wright, "BILLY BOY TOO", N. Vancouver, B.C.

HOWABOAT SHRIMP PUFFS

MAKES 24 PUFFS

1	egg white	Whip stiffly.

1/2 c	mayonnaise	Fold into egg whites.
1/4 c	shredded cheese	
1/8 t	paprika	
1/8 t	salt	
few grains	red pepper	

12	cooked shrimp	Chop shrimp and add to above.

Heap lightly onto crackers, toast rounds or miniature patty shells. Broil till light brown — serve hot.

Sophia Johnston, "ANIK", Richmond, B.C.

LAYERED CRAB DIP

8 oz pkg	cream cheese	Mix, spread in shallow serving dish.
1 T	Worcester sauce	
1 T	onion, grated	
1¹/₂ t	lemon juice	
¹/₂ c	chili sauce	Spread over top.
7 oz can	crab meat or fresh crab	Drain, rinse and spread over chili sauce.
2 T	fresh parsley	Chop and garnish.

Last minute company? Whip this up as they "come aboard".

Doris Ordano, "M/V SALISHAN", N. Vancouver, B.C.

CAPITAL CRAB DIP

8 oz can	crab meat or fresh crab	Drain.
1 c	sour cream	Mix and add to crab.
¹/₂ c	Miracle Whip	
1 T	onion, chopped	
1 T	horseradish	
2 T	parsley, chopped	
1 t	French mustard	
¹/₈ t	Worcester sauce	
to taste	Tabasco, salt and pepper	

Jocy Hanson, "SUMMER BREEZE", Tofino, B.C.

Be contented when you have all you want.

HOLBROOK JACKSON

LAKE WARAMAUG DIP — (a layered dip)

2 — 8 oz cans	jalapeno bean dip	Spread in flat bottom serving dish.
3 1 t 2 t	avocados salt lemon juice	Mash together and spread over bean dip.
1 c $^1/_2$ c 1 pkg	sour cream mayonnaise taco meat seasoning	Mix together and spread over avocado layer.
2 — 15 oz cans 2 lge 1 bunch $^1/_2$ lb	black olives tomatoes gr. onions sharp cheddar cheese, grated	Chop and mix together then spread for topping.

Angela Blanco, "RAUL", Warren, Conn.

SPINACH DIP

1 pkg	frozen spinach	Cook, drain and chop.
1 pkg 1 c 1 lb 1 sm can	Knorr's vegetable soup mayonnaise shrimp or crab, chopped water chestnuts, chopped	Mix well, add to spinach, chill. Serve with crackers or spread on small slices of French bread.

Ellen Dawes, "SEACREST", Vancouver, B.C.

THE "CRESSET"
"Cresset" built 1929, first winner of Swiftsure Race.

SALADS

For Seagoing Caesar see page 135.

A famous old saying has it that it takes four people to make a salad: a spendthrift for the oil;
                  a miser for the vinegar;
                  a judge for the salt; and
                  a madman to mix it all up.

This especially applies to green salads which are assembled from a variety of leafs from iceberg lettuce to nasturtium leaves.

The most durable of basic ingredients are featured so that you can add seafood and meats to your salad larder "as you go". A carefully selected group of salad dressings is included — standard shelf dressings such as French, Roquefort and mayonnaise are best store bought.

Salads are very "chic" aboard — easy to prepare, wholesome and easy to eat with interruptions, so there are many main course options.

Salads are the "buffer zone" of your larder as the hard vegetables, cheeses and hard sausages together with olives and other preserved items keep well and form a base.

SALAD TIPS

— For dressings prepared cold use a screw top jar and shake to blend.

— Substitute citrus juices for vinegar for variation.

— Olive oil adds a special flavour to leafy vegetables.

— Wash greens in cold water, do not soak.

— Store leafy vegetables in a towel or paper towels in the refrigerator.

— To clean tomatoes of seeds (which are bitter), quarter them and squeeze in hand — over the sink, of course.

— In leaf salads 1 T of dressing per person is usually adequate.

— Don't forget salad garnish variables such as crisp crumbled bacon, croutons, olives and shredded cabbage.

BASIC OIL & VINEGAR DRESSING & VARIATIONS

3 T	olive oil	Place all ingredients in a jar and
1 T	red wine vinegar	shake well.
to taste	salt and pepper	

Variations: Try adding one or more of the following — 1 t soy sauce; 1 t chopped green onions; 1 t toasted sesame seeds; or ¼ t dijon mustard. Use lemon juice, malt, cider or white wine vinegar instead of the red wine vinegar.

SALAD CANDICE

SERVES 4

1 sm cont.	sour cream
1 c	mini marshmallows
1 tin	mandarin oranges, drained
1 tin	pineapple chunks, drained
1 c	long shredded coconut, sweetened

Make this one the night before. Mix all ingredients together thoroughly. Serve chilled.

Cathy Fouchard, "CANTYRE", Prince George, B.C.

WALDORF SALAD

SERVES 4

1	apple, chopped	Mix together well.
1 c	celery, diced	
1 lg	orange, peeled and chopped	
1 pkg	walnuts, shelled, halved	

1 c	cream	Beat together till thick then pour over fruit and toss well. Refrigerate till ready to serve.
1 T ea.	lemon juice and sugar	
1/2 t	dry mustard	
to taste	salt and pepper	

lettuce leaves	Serve on a bed of lettuce.

Edith Thorsness, "LEILANI", Prince George, B.C.

SUMMER SALAD

SERVES 4

1	cantaloupe	Peel and dice, sprinkle with juice, salt and pepper, mix well. Serve on bed of lettuce.
2	tomatoes	
1	avocado	
	lemon juice	

Marilyn Sullivan, "MARIBU", Seattle, Wa.

EGG SALADS

Salads are a perfect summertime treat, tasty and delicious, especially with the added goodness of eggs. Chopped, sliced, grated, encased in a gelatin mold or made into a zesty dressing, eggs add spark to your salad greens. Eggs are an excellent dietary source of protein and a good source of Vitamin A, phosphorus, iron and other important nutrients. Canada's Food Guide suggests that two eggs may replace one serving of meat, fish or poultry. Egg slices or quarters, grated yolk or white are just a few ideas.

101 EGG SALAD IDEAS — With a little bit of imagination your basic egg salad recipe can look and taste truly inspired. Try the following combinations and suggested presentations. Let them be the begin-ning of your own egg salad originals.

DELICIOUS COMBINATIONS — Chopped dill and cucumber; soy sauce and green onions; chutney and almonds; cream cheese and oranges; ham and avocado; chopped nuts or seeds; smoked salmon and caviar; bacon bits and cooked spinach; shrimp/crab, dill and lemon.

DIFFERENT DRESSINGS — Rather than just mayonnaise, try using sour cream, yogurt, oil and vinegar or your favourite salad dressing to moisten.

DIFFERENT BASES — Egg salad is also marvellous on a variety of bases — try puff pastry shells, small cream puffs, tart shells, toast cases, hollowed out cucumbers, zucchinis, bell peppers, tomatoes, avocadoes, mushroom caps or snow pea pods.

THE "EGG SALAD"

8	hard cooked eggs, chopped	Mix all ingredients well. Refrigerate and use within 3 days.
$1/2$ c	mayonnaise	
$1/4$ c	celery, finely chopped	
2 T	onion, finely chopped	
1 t	Dijon mustard	
$1/4$ t	salt	
dash	pepper	

For fancier fixings, add any of the following: 4 slices crisp bacon, crumbled; $1/2$ c of chopped cook ham, raisins, slivered almonds, crushed pineapple or shredded cheese; or 1 t curry powder.

SALAD NICOISE

SERVES 4

1 c	lettuce torn	Mix together and spread in bottom of shallow salad bowl.
1 c	spinach, torn	
$1^1/2$ c	green beans, cooked	Arrange mounds of chilled vegetables and eggs alternately in a circle on the salad greens.
2 med	potatoes, cooked and sliced	
2 med	tomatoes, quartered	
4	hard-cooked eggs, quartered	
6	anchovy fillets	Garnish with chopped anchovy fillets and pour dressing over.
$1/3$ c	vinaigrette dressing	

Donna Olson, "CAROLINE", Prince George, B.C.

Get your facts first, and then you can distort them as much as you please.

MARK TWAIN

SEASIDE AMBROSIA

SERVES 4

1 lb	fresh fish fillets in 1″ cubes	Simmer in salted water till fish flakes, drain and chill.
1/2 c 1 T 4 t 2 t	mayonnaise lemon juice grated orange rind sugar	Mix together thoroughly to form dressing.
1 c 1 c 1/2 c 1/4 c	celery, thinly sliced fresh orange slices sliced ripe olives gr. onion, sliced	Combine with fish in mixing bowl, add dressing and toss lightly. Serve on lettuce leaves, avocado halves or in hollowed, lengthwise cut pineapple.

Sheila Smith, "RELIANCE", New Westminster, B.C.

SALMON CAESAR

SERVES 4

8 oz can	salmon or leftover baked salmon	Flake and set aside.
3 T 3 slices dash	vegetable oil bread, cubed garlic powder	To make croutons — saute bread in seasoned oil till crisp and golden.
1/4 c 1/4 c 1 1 t 1/2 t 1/8 t dash	vegetable oil lemon juice egg, beaten Worcester sauce salt garlic powder pepper	Assemble dressing in tightly covered jar, shake well to mix.
1 head 3 1/2 c	romaine lettuce tomatoes, diced parmesan cheese, grated	Break lettuce into salad bowl. Add croutons, salmon and tomatoes, toss lightly with dressing, sprinkle with cheese.

Raye Bowie, "LAREAL", Pender Harbour, B.C.

CUCUMBER TUNA BOATS

SERVES 6

3 sm	**cucumbers**	Cut in half lengthwise, scrape out seeds, cut small slice from bottom to steady, salt cavities.
1 can	**tuna, drained**	Combine all ingredients, fill cucumber halves, chill. Sprinkle with paprika before serving.
³/₄ c	**cheddar cheese, shredded**	
¹/₂ c	**celery, chopped**	
2	**eggs, hard boiled**	
¹/₃ c	**salad dressing**	
2 T	**sweet pickle relish**	
1 T	**onion, chopped**	
1 t	**lemon juice**	

Arlene McGinnis, "ANNIE", Tofino, B.C.

BOATERS' CUCUMBER DELIGHT

SERVES 6

3 med	**cucumbers**	Slice thinly, layer in bowl, sprinkle each layer generously with salt. Let stand at least 2 hrs. covered. Rinse with cold water, squeeze thoroughly.
1 med	**white onion**	
¹/₂ c	**sour cream**	Mix together well, toss with above in serving bowl.
to taste	**vinegar**	

Margaret Stevens, "MARLEN", N. Vancouver, B.C.

Who wishes to give himself an abundance of trouble, let him equip these two things, a ship and a woman. No two things involve more bother, for neither is ever sufficiently adorned.
PLAUTUS, Paenulus, 1. 210 (Act i, sc. 2)

TROPICAL POTATO SALAD   SERVES 4

1 c	banana circles lemon juice	Sprinkle banana with lemon juice to prevent discolouration
3 c 1 c	potatoes, cooked & diced shallots, finely chopped	Season still warm potatoes with salt & pepper, add banana slices & shallots.
1 c 2 t	mayonnaise turmeric	Blend together & pour over potatoes. Mix gently.
2	hard boiled eggs, sliced	Add & chill before serving.

PICNIC POTATO SALAD   SERVES 6-8

6 c	potatoes, cooked & cubed	Mix together
6 slices	bacon, cooked & finely chopped	
1 c	seedless cucumbers, unpeeled & diced	
2	hard cooked eggs, chopped	
1 pkg 4 c 1 T	Lipton onion soup mix sour cream vinegar	Blend together & pour over potatoes. Mix till well coated. Chill before serving.

Variation: Use to fill hollowed out tomato halves. Top with crumbled bacon & a sprig of fresh parsley.

Alane Evans, "BRANDAMBER", Tabor Lake, B.C.

There is no economy in going to bed early to save candles if the result be twins.

CHINESE PROVERB

CAULIFLOWER SALAD

SERVES 6-8

1 head	**lettuce**	Tear into bite size pieces, place in large deep dish.
³/₄ lb	**bacon, fried crisp**	Crumble bacon on top.
1 head	**cauliflower**	Break into small pieces, layer on top of bacon.
1 sm	**onion**	Slice thinly, layer on top.
1¹/₂ c	**mayonnaise**	Spread evenly over mixture.
	parmesan cheese	Sprinkle to cover top.

Cover and refrigerate overnight. Toss well just before serving.

Olga Gibson, "GIBSON GAMBLE", Vancouver, B.C.

CABBAGE KAHAGON

SERVES 6-8

1 head	**cabbage**	Shred cabbage as for coleslaw, toss together with other ingredients in serving bowl.
1 bunch	**gr. onions, sliced**	
2 cloves	**garlic, chopped**	
	toasted sesame seeds	
	chopped almonds	
1 pkg	**top Ramen noodles**	Just before serving, combine crushed noodles (without flavour packet) with other ingredients, pour over cabbage and toss well.
1 c	**oil**	
6 T	**rice vinegar**	
6 T	**sugar**	

Nan Culber, "KAHAGON", Orcas Island, Wa.

OVERNIGHT SALAD

SERVES 6

1 head	lettuce	Shred and place on bottom of large shallow serving dish.
1 pkg	frozen peas	Cook to package directions till just tender.
$^1/_2$ c 1 c 8 oz can	onion celery water chestnuts	Thinly slice onion and celery, layer on lettuce alternately with drained chestnuts and peas.
2 c 2 t $^1/_2$ c 1 t $^1/_4$ t	**Miracle Whip** **sugar** **parmesan cheese, grated** **seasoned salt** **garlic powder**	Spread Miracle Whip over. Top with mixture of remaining ingredients.
3 2 slices	**hard boiled eggs** **bacon**	Cover with sliced eggs and crisp crumbled bacon.

Cover with plastic wrap and chill overnight. Toss and garnish with tomato wedges before serving.

Betsy Buhty, "TOFINO SWELL", Tofino, B.C.

MARINATED ARTICHOKE SALAD

SERVES 4

6 oz jar 12 2 stalks 3 2 t 2 t 1 t	**artichoke hearts with liquid** **stuffed green olives, sliced** **celery, sliced** **gr. onions, chopped** **red wine vinegar** **lemon juice** **capers (optional)**	Combine all ingredients and refrigerate for 2 hrs. before serving.

Brigit Offerman, "BRIGPER", Sechelt, B.C.

GREEK SALAD AD HOC

SERVES 4

1 lg clove	garlic	Rub salad bowl with garlic, add all other ingredients.
1	English cucumber, $1/2''$ cube	
3 lg	tomatoes, $1''$ cube	
1	green pepper, $1/2''$ chop	
12	Greek olives	
1 sm	red onion, sliced	
1 c	feta cheese, crumbled	

$1/2$ c	olive oil	Mix dressing, pour over salad and toss well.
2 T	wine vinegar	
1 t	oregano	
$1/2$ t ea.	salt and pepper	

Donald Cyr, "IMAGE", Vancouver, B.C.

MARINATED PASTA SALAD

SERVES 4

$2^1/2$ c	uncooked pasta, shells or spirals	Cook, rinse and drain.

1 c	broccoli flowerets, crisp cooked	Add to pasta and chill.
$1/2$ med	red onion, sliced	
$2/3$ c	pepperoni, sliced	

$1/2$ c	vegetable oil	Mix well, refrigerate for 1 hr., pour over salad and toss.
2 T	lemon juice	
1 clove	garlic, crushed	
1 t	oregano	
$1/2$ t	dry mustard	
$1/4$ t ea.	paprika, thyme and basil	
dash	pepper	

2 med	tomatoes, wedged	Add tomatoes before serving, garnish with egg wedges.
4	hard cooked eggs	

Lou Blair, "DAEDALUS", W. Vancouver, B.C.

Artist — Joe Matzkuhn, Thetis Island, B.C.

VEGIES

Vegetables have made a comeback!! In place of their traditional role of "riding shotgun", they have been accepted as equals to the mighty meat, fish and poultry.

Often served as a separate course, they should be carefully selected and washed before preparing. The Chinese and Japanese cook vegetables quickly with plenty of seasoning and finesse. Steaming, stir frying and baking retain nutrients better than boiling.

Stuff large vegetables. Use vegetables in combination, e.g., peas and carrots, onions with spinach or Brussels sprouts.

POTATOES

Potatoes, the humblest of vegetables, yet appear on the tables of kings as well as peasants. They are a staple yet beloved by gourmets. Potatoes fill a culinary role from the most basic cooking to haute cuisine. There is no vegetable as versatile or as satisfying as the potato.

POTATO NOTES:

Potatoes can be divided into two basic types — the longer oval which is mealy textured and best baked; and the round which is harder and best boiled. Although it is possible to use any type of potato in most recipes, it is best to use an appropriate variety. The mealy oval varieties tend to fall apart when boiled and the hard round will not fluff when baked.

Store potatoes in a cool, dark place — a dry bilge is most suitable, however, potatoes kept at 70 degrees F will last a few weeks.

COOKING POTATOES

Basically, the potato is best cooked and served unpeeled. However, if peeling, do so thinly and place in cold water to prevent discolouring. When boiling, select potatoes of a uniform size or cut them into uniform size pieces. When baking, rub the skin with a little oil and pierce with a fork before cooking to allow steam to escape.

When deep frying, drop the cut pieces of potatoes in ice water and chill for half an hour. Dry with paper towels and fry in hot oil approximately 380 degrees F.

NEW POTATOES   SERVES 4

| 2 lbs | new potatoes | Scrub and pare or peel a single band of skin from around middle of each potato. Place in salted, boiling water, reduce heat and cook till tender. |
| 2 t | salt | |

$1/2$ c	butter	Toss potatoes with butter, add herbs and season to taste.
$1/4$ c	parsley chopped	
1 T	chives, chopped	

POTATO SKINS

2 lge	baking potatoes	In 400 degree oven bake till tender (app. 70 mins.). Remove and reduce oven to 375 degrees. Cool slightly, halve lengthwise scoop out potato leaving 1/4" shell, reserving scooped out potato for another use.
1 1/2 T	butter	Brush insides with melted butter,
1/2 c	cheese, grated	sprinkle in the cheese and top with
4 strips	bacon, fried and crumbled	bacon. Bake 30 mins. or until tops are golden.

Serve as a side dish or cut into strips for appetizers.

CHEESE/BACON POTATOES

SERVES 4

4 lge	baking potatoes	In 400 degree oven bake till tender (app. 70 mins.). Remove and reduce oven to 350 degrees. Cool slightly, halve lengthwise scoop out potato leaving 1/4" shell.
2 T	butter	Mash potatoes and stir in remaining
1/3 c	sour cream	ingredients. Spoon back into shells,
1/4 c	blue cheese, crumbled	return to oven and bake till heated
2 T	milk	through, approx. 20 mins.
	salt and pepper	
4 strips	bacon, fried and crumbled	Sprinkle bacon over and serve hot.

Gambling — the sure way to get nothing for something.

WILSON MIZNER

VEGIE VARIATIONS

SWEET POTATOES WITH GREEN PEPPERS *SERVES* 4

4 c	sweet potatoes	Cut potatoes in 1″ cubes and fry till crispy on outside and cooked through. Set aside.
4 c	potatoes	
6 T	vegetable oil	

1 T	mustard seed	In same pan add mustard seeds, shaking till they begin to pop.

1 c	gr. peppers 1″ sq.	Add to mustard seeds and cook stirring till peppers are still slightly crunchy. Return potatoes to pan, add salt to taste and heat through.
2 t	fennel seeds	
1 t	cumin	
1 clove	garlic	
to taste	salt	

JULIENNE BEETS *SERVES* 4

15 oz can	beets, julienned	Mix ingredients together gently and heat through.
1/4 c	whipping cream	
1 t	dijon mustard	
1/2 t	parsley	

CREAMED VEGIES

1/2 c	butter	Melt butter over low heat, add flour and cook stirring till lightly brown.
1/2 c	flour	

2 c	whole milk	Whisk in, cook and stir till smooth and thick. Bring to boil. Pour over any cooked vegies and mix gently.
1/2 t	salt	
1/4 t	white pepper	

Serious vegetarians will, of course, have their own meal plans whereby vegetables are carefully complemented by grains, seeds, etc., to obtain complete protein. They certainly travel in good company — Plato, Socrates, Isaac Newton, Benjamin Franklin, Brigitte Bardot and Raquel Welch are all wonderful examples of vegetarians.

Fisherman at Dawn
Ruth, Julie, Arvez and Red Snapper in Acapulco.

ONIONS

"... Our present anchorage was much exposed, and supplied us with no sort of refreshment except a few small wild onions or leeks." So saith the "DISCOVERY" log while Vancouver was in the Gulf Islands in the spring of 1792.

Onions are more than a simple flavouring. This orthodox vegetable can be elevated to right guard to create a delicious meal. There is no question about it the earthy onion is the most important vegetable in my kitchen. It can be chopped, shredded, sliced, diced. It can be sauteed, stuffed, boiled, blanched, braised or baked. As a flavouring agent it adds depth to soups, stocks, stews and sauces.

When cooked, its flavour is transposed from crisp and zesty to rich and sweet. When sauteed in olive oil or butter, a tantalizing, sweet aroma fills the galley.

A note of caution — your eyes won't water if onions are chilled before slicing, dicing or shredding.

CRISPY ONION RINGS

$^2/_3$ c	flour	Mix together dry ingredients. Add water, whisk rapidly till smooth. Refrigerate for 1 hr.
$^1/_3$ c	cornstarch	
$^1/_4$ t	salt	
1 c	ice water	
$^1/_2$ t	baking soda	Remove above from refrigerator and whisk in soda.
	vegetable oil	Heat $2^1/_2$" oil in wok to 375 degrees.
2 lg	onions, sliced	

Coat onion rings in batter and drop one by one into hot oil. Fry till crispy brown (1 min.). Remove with slotted spoon, place on paper towel, sprinkle with salt and keep warm till all are done. Serve hot.

STUFFED ONIONS

4 med.	onions	Peel, cook in salted water till tender, drain and cool. Remove inside leaving 1/4″ shell.
4 T	butter	Chop innards and saute lightly.
1/2 c 1/2 c 1/4 c	cooked ham, chopped Swiss cheese, grated dijon mustard white wine	Mix together with sauted onion, stuff in onion casings and moisten with wine.
1 c	chicken broth	Place onions in casserole dish and pour chicken broth around. Bake at 375 degrees for 20 mins.
4 slices	Swiss cheese	Place on top of onions and bake till cheese is melted.

SWEET & SOUR ONIONS

(use as a sauce for pork, chicken, etc.)

1/3 c 1/2 c	raisins brandy	Place in saucepan, bring to simmer, remove and set aside for 30 mins.
1 1/2 lb 2 T	small white boiling onions (about 24) olive oil	Trim ends of onions and remove outer layer. Saute over med. heat shaking pan till speckled all over (about 5 mins.).
1 T	sugar	Sprinkle on sugar tossing for 3 mins. to carmelize.
16 oz can 2 T 1/2 t ea. 1/4 t	tomatoes cider vinegar salt and thyme pepper	Add tomatoes with juice, reserved raisins and remaining ingredients. Break up tomatoes, bring to boil over med. heat, scraping bottom of pan to bring up caramelized sugar.

Pour over chicken or pork chops in baking dish. Seal tightly with aluminum foil. Bake for 1 3/4 hours at 350 degrees.

ART'S CHILI-TEQUILA VEGIES — 37 WAYS

I use ORTEGO chilis — I hope they don't mind! (always have a can on board)

BASICS — 2 cans (14 oz) vegies
1 can (4 oz) mild chili diced
Select herb, stir and heat

VARIABLES — ¼ c sour cream and/or 1 T tequila

HERB		JUDGMENT
R — Rosemary	⅛ T	G — Good
O — Oregano	⅛ T	M — Mmmm
A — Anise	¼ T	E — Excellent
S — Savory	½ T	X — Not recommended
T — Tarragon	½ T	

		SELECT HERB	BASIC	ADD SOUR CREAM	ADD TEQUILA ONLY	ADD SOUR CREAM & TEQUILA
Beans	— Green	R	G	G	G	E
	— Yellow	S	M	G	G	E
	— Lima	T	G	M	G	E
	— Kidney	S	G	M	M	E
Beets	— Julienne	O	M	E	M	EE
Carrots	— Sliced	A	M	X	X	X
Corn	— Kernel	S	G	G	M	E
Peas	— Petit	R	G	M	M	E
	— Snow	S	G	G	G	M
Spinach	— chopped	A	G	M	G	E*

*Makes an excellent dip.

Notes: Add sour cream just prior to serving.
Add tequila after sour cream.
Use equal amounts of canned/fresh/frozen vegetables.
Add bacon bits or sesame seeds for variation.

For Fun: Start with basic and sour cream — add tequila for seconds.

Leftovers: Can't tell you — we never have any.

Not judged by a 'panel of judges'. Let me know if this doesn't work.

STOVE TOP

"THE EMERALD SEA", SCUBA AND CIOPINI

It takes a big ling cod to satisfy boaters and divers alike after a day on or under the sea.

It is easy to see why Powell River is the diving capital of Canada with Desolation Sound, Jervis Inlet, Egmont and innumerable other well known sites all within a 20-mile radius.

National Geographic's 26-page multi-photo'd article of April 1980 described the area as "The Cold Emerald Sea" and it is just that to divers from around the world. Jim Willoughby, renowned diving director of the Beach Gardens Resort, Powell River, guides diving visitors on unforgettable dive tours. When they arrive back "home" Head Chef David Bowes has a steaming pot of his Ciopini ready. The big ling cod shown in Jim's undersea photo with singer Terry Jack's wife, Margret, later graced one of David's pots. He invites you all to try his Ciopini recipe, page 86.

OYSTER STEW

4 T	butter	Saute oysters in butter till they curl
2 c	oysters, shucked and chopped	(3-4 mins.).
8	gr. onions, chopped	Add to oysters.
1 t ea.	Lawrey's salt and paprika	
$^1/_2$ t	pepper	
4 c	milk, scalded	Add to oysters, bring just to boil.

Garnish with parsley, onion tops and butter.

Clare Rainer, "BLUE SKY NO. 1", Hopkins Landing, B.C.

COD PROVENCALE

$^1/_2$ c	butter	Saute garlic and onions in butter for a
1 clove	garlic, chopped	few mins.
$1^1/_2$ t	gr. onions, chopped	
$^1/_2$ c	tomatoes, peeled, seeded, chopped	Add to garlic mixture, simmer 5 mins. or till liquid is reduced slightly.
$^1/_4$ c	dry white wine	Keep warm.
1 t	parsley, chopped	
$^1/_4$ t ea.	salt and thyme	
$^1/_2$	bay leaf	
pinch	pepper	
2 lbs	cod or snapper fillets, boned and skinned	Dip fillets in egg, then in flour, shake off excess flour. Heat butter and oil
2	eggs, beaten well	over med. heat in large frying pan,
$^3/_4$ c	flour	cook fillets 10 mins. per inch
$^1/_4$ c	butter	thickness, turning once. Pour sauce
2 T	olive oil	over fish and serve.

Andrea Barnes, "LADY ANDREA", Gibsons, B.C.

CURRIED SHRIMP

SERVES 4

5 T	butter	Saute onions in butter till tender.
$^1/_2$ c	onions, chopped	
6 T	flour	Add to onions, stirring constantly.
1-3 t	curry powder	
1$^1/_2$ t	sugar	
1 t	salt	
$^1/_4$ t	ginger	
1 cube	chicken bouillon	Dissolve cube in water, add to
1 c	boiling water	onions, stir till thickened.
2 c	milk	Add to above, heat through but do
1 t	lemon juice	not boil.
1 lb	shrimp meat	

Jocey Hanson, "SUMMER BREEZE", Tofino, B.C.

SELMA PARK SAUCY COD

SERVES 4

1 lb	cod or snapper fillets	Simmer fillets in milk till they flake
1 c	milk	easily, remove and drain. Set fish aside.
$^1/_2$ c	milk	Mix together, add to hot milk and
2 T	cornstarch	cook till thickened.
$^1/_2$ c	shrimp meat	Return fillets to pan, add shrimp and
dash	Worcester sauce	seasonings, heat through.
to taste	salt and pepper	

Diana Gruner, "THE CROW'S NEST", Gibsons, B.C.

ARLENE'S PRAWNS SUPREME

SERVES 4-6

3 lbs	prawns	Cook, shell and set aside.
	vegetable oil	Saute till soft.
1 clove	garlic, crushed	
1/3 c	gr. pepper, chopped	
3	gr. onions, chopped	
2 stalks	celery, chopped	
	flour	Add to thicken.
1 can	chicken bouillon	Stir in bouillon undiluted, cook till thickened, flavour to taste.
few		
drops	tabasco and soya	
	cream	Just before serving add cream and prawns, heat through but do not boil.

Arlene McGinnis, "ANNIE", Tofino, B.C.

KEDGEREE

SERVES 4

This dish which originated in India from a dish called "khicharhi" was most likely brought to the west coast by the worldly navigators of the Capt. George Vancouver era.

1/2 c	rice, raw	Prepare rice to just before tenderness, drain.
1 lb	fillet of cod or salmon	Cook fillets in boiling water just long enough to set flakes, drain and break into large pieces.
2 T	butter	Melt butter in pan, add rice and fish, salt to taste. Pour milk over and heat on low till milk is absorbed, about 5 mins.
to taste	salt	
1/2 c	milk	
2-3	eggs, boiled	Mix lightly with fork, garnish with egg slices and parsley.
	parsley, chopped	

Neil Campbell, "BUBBLES", Sechelt, B.C.

GYPSY CLAM PASTA

3 T	olive oil	Saute.
2 cloves	garlic, crushed	

3 stalks	celery, chopped	Add, saute till barely tender.
2	gr. onions, chopped	
1	tomato, chopped	
2 T	parsley	
1 sm	zucchini, sliced	
$^1/_3$ c	mushrooms, sliced	

$^1/_2$ c	clams, canned or fresh with liquid	Add and simmer for a few mins.
3 T	white wine	
to taste	salt and pepper	

$^1/_2$ lb	pasta, cooked	Serve clam sauce over hot pasta, top
	Parmesan or Romano cheese	with grated cheese.

Meryn Rosback, "GYPSY V", Alert Bay, B.C.

OYSTERS IN SOYA BATTER

2	eggs	Mix together thoroughly.
$^3/_4$ c	flour	
$^1/_4$ c ea.	water and soya sauce	
to taste	ginger and garlic	

	oysters	Dip oysters in above batter, fry in hot oil till cooked on both sides.

Sharon Palm, "WRECK CHECKER", Tofino, B.C.

UP ON EGGS

Eggs are food for all hours, all seasons and all iceboxes (and refrigerators). Of all fresh foods, eggs store the easiest and longest.

Uncooked	Refrigerated	1 Week or More
Cooked (in/out shell)	Refrigerated	Up to 1 week

In form, artists say the egg approaches perfection; as food, we tend to treat the egg lightly. We take the egg for granted as commonly as the coy claim, "Well, I can boil an egg". In fact, eggs should not be boiled — high temperatures and prolonged heat exposure causes the egg whites to turn tough. The way not to cook an egg is to "pluck" it out of the "ice box" into a pot of boiling water. To cook eggs in the shell THE COLD METHOD put in a saucepan and cover with cool water. Place over high heat, cover and bring up to boil. Remove from heat and let stand 2-5 mins. for soft, 15-20 mins. for hard cooked. Take out hard cooked immediately and put under cold running water to facilitate shell removal.

For those who prefer THE HOT METHOD, try this: lower eggs into boiling water, remove from heat, cover, let stand for 6-8 mins. for soft and 20-25 mins. for hard cooked. Cool soft cooked in cold water to stop cooking. Cool hard cooked for easy shell removal. Now that you've got boiled (oops!) cooked eggs in hand, let's look at:

POACHED — Use the freshest eggs and slide into barely simmering water about 2" deep for 3-5 mins. Drain well. Do not add vinegar — it doesn't help.

STEAM POACHED — Cook in buttered ramekins with 1" of water.

SCRAMBLED — Cook at moderate temperature in non-stick pan allowing 2 eggs per serving. Mix with salt and pepper and 1 T of water or milk per egg. Pour egg mixture into a buttered pan, stirring occasionally until cooked throughout but still moist. Try some of the following for variations to plain scrambled eggs:

— When partially cooked, add grated cheese (Mmmm), diced ham, mushrooms, canned shrimp, peppers or chilies (mild), chopped celery and a herb or your favourite seasoning;

— Top with shredded cheese;

— When partially cooked, stir in cubes of cream cheese;

— Add crumbled, cooked bacon or sauteed chopped onions or cubed avocados.

FRIED — Whether sunny side up or once over lightly (firm white) eggs should be fried at low to medium temperatures to avoid rubbery whites and leathery undersides.

STEAM FRIED — In moderately hot pan break and slip in eggs — when whites begin to set, add 1 teaspoon of water per egg, cover and cook for 4-6 mins.

FAT FRIED — In a moderately hot pan break and slip in eggs — cook slowly, basting or turning to cook both sides (break yolk before turning if using in a sandwich).

Oh, by the way — when Ruth cooks hard boiled eggs and identification of the carton is a problem, I spin them — raw eggs wobble, cooked ones don't!!

Never work before breakfast; if you have to work before breakfast, have breakfast first.

JOSH BILLINGS

SPEEDI-SPANISH OMELETTE — SERVES 1

1 t	butter	For the filling, saute onions and green pepper till partially cooked.
1 T	onion, chopped	
2 T	gr. pepper, chopped	
1/3 c	tomato sauce	Add to above, simmer and stir frequently 5-10 mins.
1/2 t	Worcester sauce	
2	eggs	Combine with fork — avoid over-beating.
1 T	water	
to taste	salt and pepper	

METHOD #1   Filling may be mixed in with eggs; or

METHOD #2   Fold egg mixture into heated pan (med/high), add filling just before folding over.

BATTERS AND FRITTERS

You can "toy" with these basic batters even though they're simply among the best. For deep frying, a stiff mix is more successful. For seafoods, mix chopped celery or onions for flavourful variations; for fruits, add sugar and lemon juice in varying degrees depending on tartness.

Fritters are a light and crisp change to your boating fare. Presented as an appetizer or main dish they are a galley delight. Cooking fritters as a "pancake" is a very acceptable galley alternative. The mix should be somewhat stiffer than pancake mix to form in the skillet to about $3/8"$ to $1/2"$ thick. Adjust liquids or vary ingredients to achieve consistency. For example, reduce flour to half and replace liquid with a 10 oz can of creamed corn for Corn Fritters. Hmm . . . this is fun! How about corn and clams? A touch of curry to shrimp?

BETTER BASIC BATTER   SERVES 4

1 c	flour	Combine.
$1/4$ t	salt	
2 t	vegetable oil	Add and blend. Refrigerate 30 mins.
$1^1/_3$ c	cold water	
2	egg whites	Beat stiff, fold in just before using.

BEER BATTER   SERVES 4

1	egg	Beat egg and add flat beer to make
1 bottle	flat beer	1 c total.
$3/4$ c	flour	Add, let stand 10 mins., stir and it's
1 T	baking powder	ready to use.
1 t	sugar	

Jean Rowledge, "CAPT. CRUNCH", Gibsons, B.C.

LORNE'S 'SECRET' PAN-FRY

SERVES 4

Designed for the health conscious chef who wishes to avoid extra calories and cholesterol usually associated with the frying process. May be used for many seafoods.

2 lbs	fish fillets whole or portion cornstarch	In plastic bag shake fillets with starch and your favourite spices.
	cold pressed safflower oil or other oil	Heat oil in bottom of pan till hot but not smoking, add fish, turn when golden brown.

Serve with lemon wedges on paper towel lined platter.

Lorne Berman, "M/V OAK", Secret Cove, B.C.

CLAM FRITTERS

SERVES 4

1 c	flour	Mix together.
1/4 t	salt	
1/8 t	pepper	
1/4 c ea.	milk and clam liquor	Combine, discarding remaining clam liquor and mix into flour.
2	eggs, beaten	
10 oz can	clams	Add and mix. Drop by tablespoon into hot oil till brown, turn.

Meryn Rosback, "GYPSY V", Alert Bay, B.C.

JULIE'S HEAVENLY HOTS

SERVES 4

1 c	sour cream	Mix together well.
3 T	flour	
1 1/2 T	sugar	
2	eggs, beaten	
1/2 t	baking soda	

Drop dollar size spoonfuls on griddle (hot and fast). Turn.

Julie Jones, "JULIE J", Los Angeles, Ca.

CHILI

Chili is Texan, they say — hearty, spicy and sociable. Chili societies are springing up all over and cookoffs are an occasion and a ritual at which cool beer and margaritas complement. Aspirant masters fuss over their bubbling pots like witches.

Purists say "real" chili has no beans but whether you like yours "beaned" or not, remember this is "cornball" not "haute cuisine", providing clean fun with a sense of camaraderie.

Invite your neighbour — chili warms the palate as well as the conversation. A word of caution though — chili powders vary in strength so add slowly to avoid warming the palate more than was intended.

MIKE'S CHILI

SERVES 4

1 lb	beef chuck	Cube beef, dry, toss in paprika,
1/2 t	paprika	brown in oil.
1 med	onion, chopped	Remove beef, set on one side. In
1 clove	garlic, finely chopped	same pan saute onions and garlic.
14 oz can	tomatoes	Combine all ingredients, including beef, simmer till meat is tender. Beer
5 oz can	tomato paste	instead of water adds pleasant
1 T	chili (or to taste)	flavour.
1/2 t ea.	cumin and oregano	
	beer or water as req'd. to moisten	

When serving, garnish to taste with chopped red or green peppers, onion, tomato, green chilies, sour cream, cooked kidney beans.

Mike McGinnis, "NOR'WESTER", Porpoise Bay, B.C.

CHICKEN CHILI

1/4 c	margarine	Saute till tender.
1 stalk	celery, chopped	
2 cloves	garlic	
15 oz can	whole tomatoes	Stir in, cook uncovered till reduced slightly.
2 c	chicken broth	
6 oz can	ortego chilies	
2 T	chili powder	
1 t	ground cumin	
1/2 t ea.	thyme and oregano	
2 c	cooked chicken, cubed	Stir in and heat through. Serve with hot minute rice.

Greg Evans, "DURANT I", Prince George, B.C.

AMBER'S SPEEDI CHILI

3 T	vegetable oil	Saute till tender.
2 med	onions, chopped	
1 clove	garlic	
1 lb	lean ground beef	Stir in, cook till brown.
14 oz can	kidney beans, drained	Add and cook uncovered 20 mins. or till heated through.
1 stick	pepperoni, chopped	
14 oz can	tomatoes	
2 t ea.	oregano and chili powder	
1 t ea.	cumin and paprika	
	beer to moisten	

Shirley Marsh, "WE'LL SEA", Vancouver, B.C.

CHICKEN TETRAZZINI

2 T	butter	Bone and skin chicken and cut into
2	chicken breasts	1″ strips, fry till brown.
15 med	mushrooms, sliced	Add and saute till tender.
1¹/₂ c	chicken bouillon	Add ³/₄ c bouillon and remaining
¹/₄ c	dry white wine	ingredients to chicken and simmer.
	or rye	Set aside.
to taste	salt and pepper	
¹/₄ c	butter	Melt butter, blend in flour till smooth.
¹/₄ c	flour	Add milk and remaining bouillon, stir
¹/₂ c	milk	on med. heat till thick. Add chicken and heat.
¹/₂ c	cheddar cheese, grated	Add and stir till melted. Pour over noodles and serve.

Olga Gibson, "GIBSONS GAMBLE", Vancouver, B.C.

SKILLET HAM SALAD

1 T	vegetable oil	Cook together, stirring, till lightly
¹/₄ c	gr. onions, chopped	browned.
¹/₄ c	gr. peppers, chopped	
2 c	ham, diced	
3 c	cooked potatoes, diced	Add, heat and mix lightly.
¹/₄ c	mayonnaise	
to taste	salt and pepper	
1¹/₂ c	sharp cheese, diced	Stir in cheese till it begins to melt.

Garnish with chopped green onions or parsley.

Lis Matzkuhn, "AMBER", Thetis Island, B.C.

NEW ENGLAND DINNER

2 T	butter	Saute onion in butter till tender then
$^1/_2$ c	onion, chopped	add carrots, cover and cook over low
2 c	carrots, pared and sliced	heat 10 mins.
2	potatoes, cooked and cubed	Add to onions, cover and cook 10 mins. or till cabbage is tender.
4 c	cabbage, shredded	
$^1/_2$ lb	corned beef, cooked and cut in strips	
$^1/_2$ t ea.	dry mustard, thyme and salt	
1	bay leaf	
$^1/_8$ t	pepper	

Nan Culver, "KAHAJON", Orcas Island, Wa.

POLISH SAUSAGE/POTATO SKILLET

SERVES 4

1 can	cream of mushroom soup	Heat in skillet, mixing well.
1 sm can	milk	
$^1/_3$ c	water	
$^1/_4$ c	onion, chopped	
to taste	salt and pepper	
3 c	raw potatoes, thinly sliced	Add to skillet mixture, cover and cook on low 30 mins. or till vegies
1 c	raw carrots, sliced	are tender. Stir occasionally.
1	Polish sausage ring	Cut into 4 parts, add to skillet, cover and cook 15 mins. more.

Ann Weaver, "LA TORTUGA", Lodi, Ca.

HOT CAESAR CONSOMME

48 oz can	**clamato juice**	Mix in large pan and simmer 15-20 mins.
10 oz can	**beef consomme**	
1 c	**canned tomatoes, drained and chopped**	
3 T	**lemon juice**	

Season with Worcester, tabasco, salt and pepper. Garnish with celery salt. Option: put 1 oz vodka in mug before adding soup.

Fran Grandbois, "GOONIE BIRD", Vancouver, B.C.

BEACH GARDEN CIOPINI   SERVES 8-10

3 T	**butter**	In a heavy bottomed soup pot saute finely chopped onions and garlic, celery and mushrooms.
1/2 med	**onion, chopped**	
3 cloves	**garlic, chopped**	
1/2 stalk	**celery**	
1/2 lb	**mushrooms, sliced**	
6 oz can	**tomato paste**	Add and continue to saute.
19 oz can	**tomatoes, broken up**	Add and simmer for 1/2 hr.
36 oz	**tomato juice**	
4 oz	**dry red wine**	
2 T	**fresh basil, chopped**	
1 T	**salt**	
1 t	**pepper**	
1/2	**gr. pepper, diced**	Add and simmer another 1/2 hr.
1 lb	**ling cod or snapper**	Cut fish in 1" cubes. 1/2 hr. before serving add seafood all together and simmer.
1/2 lb	**salmon**	
1/2 lb	**clams or mussels in shell**	
1/4 lb	**prawns, peeled**	
1/4 lb	**scallops**	

Serve in large soup plates garnished with parsley.

Head Chef David Bowes, BEACH GARDEN RESORT, Powell River, B.C.

GALLEY BOUILLABAISSE

2 T	olive oil	Saute till brown and tender.
1	onion, sliced	
1 clove	garlic, minced	
1	bay leaf	
1/4 t	thyme	
1 can	tomato soup	Add, bring to boil, cover and simmer
1 soup can	water	5 mins.
2 c	cooked seafood, crab, fish, shrimp	
1 t	lemon juice	
dash	tabasco	
4 slices	French bread, toasted	Place toast in bowl and cover with bouillabaisse.

Vivian Chamberlin, "SUMMER GOLD", Gibsons, B.C.

VIKING CHOWDER

3 T	butter	In large pot saute till soft but not
1 lg	onion, sliced	browned.
3 T	flour	Quickly stir in flour and blend, then
2 c	chicken broth	add broth and tomatoes, cook and
28 oz can	stewed tomatoes	stir till thickened.
1/2 lb	cooked crab meat or mock crab	Add and simmer 5 mins. or till heated through. Freezes well.
1/2 lb	cooked shrimp	

1921 heritage wooden tugboat picture (over).

Dorothy Mackenzie, "VIKING KING", Port Coquitlam, B.C.

1921 Heritage Tug "Viking King" — (Recipe p. 89).

UP ON ROASTING

George Bernard Shaw is quoted, "If the British can survive their meals, they can survive anything". This may well have been the beginning of "The Roast". In defence of the British, here is

Yorkshire Pudding:

| 1 c ea. | flour and milk | Sift flour and salt, add milk |
| 1/4 t | salt | gradually. |

| 2 | eggs, unbeaten | Add eggs, whisk 2 mins. |

Chill 1 hr. Cover bottom of preheated baking or muffin pans with roast drippings, pour in batter 3/4" deep, bake at 450 degrees till risen. Lower to 375 degrees and cook till brown.

ROASTING CHART			Oven Temp.		Meat Temp.		Approx. Min/lb.
	Rare				140F	60C	18-20
BEEF	Medium		300F	150C	160F	71C	23-25
	Well Done				170F	77C	27-30
VEAL	Well Done		300F	150C	170F	77C	25-30
LAMB			300F	150C	180F	83C	30-35
PORK	Small Roasts		350F	180C	185F	85C	30-35
	Butt						50-55
HAM	Small	9-12 lb	300F	150C	150F	66C	22-25
(Smoked)	Large	12-20 lb					18-20
		3 1/2 lb					30
POULTRY		3 1/2-10 lb	325F	160C	190F	88C	20-25
		10-18 lb					18-20

PAULINE'S SECRET

1 lb	ground beef	Brown beef with other ingredients.
1 med	onion, chopped	Add salt and pepper to taste.
1/2 lb	mushrooms, sliced	
1 med	green pepper, chopped	

14 oz		Add to beef mixture and heat
can	stewed tomatoes	through.
1/2 c	Kraft catalina dressing	
1 1/2 c	cooked macaroni	

Can be put into a casserole dish, topped with cheese and baked at 350 degrees for 20 mins.

Pauline Webber, "MOOMBA", Hopkins Landing, B.C.

EASY SPAGHETTI CASSEROLE   SERVES 4

1 fistful	spaghetti	Cook till tender in boiling, salted water.

1 med	onion, chopped	Saute onion in large skillet. Add
1 lb	ground beef	beef, brown and drain.

28 oz		Add to beef and cook for 10 mins.
can	tomatoes	
1/4 t ea.	curry and chili	
	ripe olives	
	salt and pepper	

1 c	cooked peas	Mix in peas, 1/2 of cheese and all of
1 1/2 c	cheese, grated	spaghetti.

Pour into a greased casserole, sprinkle the rest of cheese on top. Bake at 400 degrees for 30 mins.

Jean Ambrose, "M/V CHANGI", W. Vancouver, B.C.

HALIBUT — SULLIVAN BAY

SERVES 4-6

2-15 oz cans	spinach, drained and chopped	Mix together and spread in casserole dish.
to taste	mushrooms	
1 T	lemon juice	

2 lbs	halibut pieces	Dip fish in egg and lemon juice mixture.
1	egg, beaten	
1 T	lemon juice	

	bread crumbs	Coat fish with bread crumb mixture and lay over spinach.
	parmesan cheese	
	pepper and garlic	

½ c	sour cream	Mix together, spread over top of fish. Bake at 375 degrees for 30 mins or till fish flakes.
½ c	mayonnaise	
1½ c	cheddar cheese, grated	
4	green onions, chopped	
1 T	lemon juice	

Lynn Whitehead, SULLIVAN BAY MARINE RESORT, B.C.

BAKED SALMON AND TARRAGON SAUCE

3 lb	salmon	Smear fish with butter, salt, pepper, lemon juice and parsley. Cover and bake at 425 degrees 10 mins. per inch. Baste. Keep warm on serving dish.
1 T	butter, softened	
1	lemon	
to taste	salt and pepper	
	parsley	

SAUCE

4 T	butter	Combine in small pot and bring just to boil. Remove from heat and add 4 T of salmon cooking liquid. Pour some sauce over salmon and serve rest separately.
1½ T	white wine	
1 t	tarragon	
1 t	soya sauce	
to taste	salt and pepper	

Becky Beaton, "VERACITY", Gibsons, B.C.

WILD RICE CASSEROLE (or regular rice) — SERVES 8-10

2	onions, chopped	Combine thoroughly. Can use
1″ cube	ginger, fresh	regular or wild rice.
$^1/_2$ c	parsley, chopped	
7 oz can	tomato sauce	
4 c	rice, cooked	
$^1/_4$ c	oil	Heat oil, add seeds and stir for 30
1 t	cumin seeds	secs. Add to above mixture and mix
1 t	fennel seeds	well.
$^1/_8$ t	fenugreek seeds	
$^1/_4$ c	apricots, chopped	Add to above and mix well. Put in
$^1/_4$ c	pine nuts	casserole and bake for 1 hr. at 350
$^1/_4$ c	raisins	degrees F.
1 t	sugar	
1 t	lemon juice	
dash ea.	salt and pepper	

Barbara and Norm Corbett, "SHIBUMI", Gibsons, B.C.

HONEY CURRY CHICKEN — SERVES 4

for 4	finger size chicken pieces	
$^1/_3$ c	margarine	Mix together in baking dish and coat
$^1/_3$ c	honey	chicken pieces. Bake at 350 degrees
2 T	curry	till cooked through.
3 T	French mustard	

Bake uncovered for finger eating or covering dish will retain liquids to form sauce for rice, etc.

Philly Robb, "GIBSONS MARINA", Calgary, Alta.

HERBED SALMON

SERVES 4

1¹/₂ lb	salmon fillets or steaks	Place skin side down in shallow pan.
1 T	butter	Saute shallots over med. heat 2-3
2	shallots, chopped	mins. Stir in lemon juice and
1 T	lemon juice	marjoram. Spoon over salmon,
3 T	dry white wine	cover with foil and bake 15-17 mins.
³/₄ t	marjoram	per inch thickness at 425 degrees or
		till opaque.

Jan Hightower, "ATOCHA", Seattle, Wa.

HOT CRAB "BREAD"

SERVES 6

1 loaf	Italian bread (12-15″ long)	Cut bread in half lengthwise and butter both sides. Cover with cheese.
¹/₄ lb	Swiss cheese	
3¹/₂ oz	crab meat, canned or fresh	Mix together, spread over cheese and bake and 350 degrees for 20-25 mins. or till brown.
¹/₄ c	mayonnaise	
¹/₄ c	sour cream	
2 T	parsley, chopped	
2 T	lemon juice	

Ellen Dawes, "SEACREST", Vancouver, B.C.

Fishing is a . . . discipline in the equality of men — for all men are equal before fish.

HERBERT HOOVER

SUNSHINE COAST PRAWNS

SERVES 4

2 lb	prawns, preferably with heads on
1 c	olive oil
1 c	sherry or red wine or combination
2 T	oregano
4 cloves	garlic, minced
3	lemons — juice only
	parsley, chopped
	salt and pepper

Combine all ingredients, coating prawns well. Bake in as large a pan as fits your boat oven, 450 degrees for 20 mins. or till pink. Turn frequently.

Diane Anderson, "MAQUINNA PT.", Sechelt, B.C.

BOTTOM FISH DISH

SERVES 4

7	fillets, deboned (cod, snapper)
2 cans	mushroom soup
3 c	cheese, grated
to taste	pepper, cracked

Cover bottom of pan with 1/2 can mushroom soup. Place 3 fillets on top and sprinkle with 1 c cheese. Continue with layers ending with mushroom soup and remaining cheese. Cover and cook 325 degrees for 20 mins. then uncover and cook 5 mins.

Pat Mawer, "EXODUS", Bellevue, Wa.

FREESTYLE BUFFET SALMON

salmon fillets	Leave skin on fillets, debone by hand or tweezers.
lemon juice **Hy's seasoning salt**	Lay fillets on broiling pan, skin side down and pour on lemon juice. Sprinkle generously with Hy's.
mayonnaise	Spread $1/4''$ thick over top and sides.
lemon pepper **dill weed (opt.)**	Sprinkle on till "black".

Broil until brownish-black on top. If fillet extra thick bake further 10 mins.

Norma Jamieson, "FREESTYLE", Richmond, B.C.

IRISH WHEATEN BREAD

3 c	whole wheat flour	Mix.
$1/2$ c	natural bran	
3 T	oatmeal	
2 t	baking powder	
1 t	baking soda	
1 t	salt	
1 c	water	Mix, add gently to above till moist.
1 c	milk	Do not over-mix.

If necessary add extra liquid as texture should be moist. Spoon into loaf pan, bake at 400 degrees 1 hr. Raisins, nuts or other grains may be added.

Mervyn Hempenstall, "CONSTANTIA", Vancouver, B.C.

BEER BREAD

1	egg	Whip egg well, add sugar, beer and half of flour mixing well. Slowly add remaining flour, whipping after each addition. Pour into greased loaf pan. Bake 350 degrees for 1 hr.
3 T	sugar	
1 bottle	beer (room temp.)	
3 c	flour	

For variation try adding nuts, raisins, cheese, etc.

Gloria la Grandeur, "GLORY", Gibsons, B.C.

DORIS' SEAFOOD MUFFINS   SERVES 6

1 c	shrimp, crab or tuna	Drain and coarsely chop.
$^1/_4$ c	cheddar cheese, grated	Add to seafood and set aside.
$^1/_3$ c	sour cream	
$^1/_4$ c	celery, finely chopped	
1$^1/_2$ c	flour	Mix and make well in centre.
2 T	white sugar	
2 t	baking powder	
$^1/_2$ t	salt	
$^1/_4$ t	thyme	
1	egg	Beat well, add to dry ingredients and stir just till moist. Spoon into greased muffin cups and top with 1 T of seafood mixture. Bake at 375 degrees for 20 mins. Serve warm garnished with fresh parsley.
$^3/_4$ c	milk	
$^1/_3$ c	oil	

Doris Davis, "JULIE D.", MacLeod, Alta.

BRENT'S BREAD

2 pkg	Pillsbury buttermilk biscuits	Evenly overlap dough in pan sprinkling cheese throughout.
1/2 c	cheddar cheese, grated	
1/4 c	butter, melted	Pour over top.

Cook according to package directions then reduce heat and cook another 10 mins. or so till golden on top and cooked through. First sampled aboard Brent Davies' "SEQUOIA PARK". It's incredibly simple and delicious — great on a cold day. Very opulent for breakfast.

Judy Killam, SECRET COVE MARINA, Secret Cove, B.C.

FRASER CANYON BANNOCK

1 c	flour	Mix together.
1 c	whole wheat flour	
1 T	baking powder	
2 T	brown sugar	
1/2 t	salt	
2 T	lard	Cut in till mixture resembles fine crumbs.
2/3 c	water	Sprinkle a little at a time till soft dough forms. Knead 10 times on floured board. Roll or pat to 1/2" circle.

Bake at 450 degrees for 10-15 mins. on greased sheet. Cut in wedges and serve hot with butter.

Jeanne Spinnelli, "JEANNE M", Victoria, B.C.

SYLVIA'S SOUR DOUGH RECIPES

SOUR DOUGH STARTER

Method #1: Scrounge ¹/₂ c starter from a friend. Add equal amounts of flour and water and 1 t sugar. Mix in non-metal pot, cover loosely, leave in warm place until it smells sour (2-3 days). Stir down, refrigerate or freeze for later use. Bring to room temperature before using.

Method #2: Combine 1¹/₂ t active yeast, 2 c flour, 2 T sugar and 2¹/₂ c warm water. Leave in warm place . . . and so on as above.

Dried crystals are also available in specialty stores.

SOUR DOUGH BISCUITS

1¹/₂ c	flour	Cut butter into dry ingredients. Add sugar and egg (if using) and sour dough starter. Knead 3-4 times, roll ³/₄″ thick and cut into biscuits. Put on ungreased cookie sheet and bake at 450 for 12-15 mins. Can also be cooked in covered heavy frying pan over medium heat, turning once.
2 t	baking powder	
¹/₂ t	baking soda	
¹/₂ t	salt	
¹/₄ c	butter or marg.	
1 T	sugar (optional)	
1	egg (optional)	
1 c	sour dough starter	

Variations: Add one or more of: bits of bacon, cheese, chili powder, sauteed onion, parsley, paprika, raisins.

SOUR DOUGH HOT CAKES

1 c	sour dough starter	Mix together. Leave in warm place overnight.
2 c	flour	
2 c	warm milk	

2	eggs	Next morning, add to sour dough mixture. Cook on lightly oiled griddle turning once.
3 T	shortening, melted	
1 T	sugar	
1 t	salt	
2 t	baking soda	

Sylvia Wallace, "OLFNEG", Calgary, Alta.

JACONA CURRY

1 lg	frying chicken, cut up	Place chicken in single layer in baking pan and sprinkle with paprika. Set aside.
1 T	paprika	

1/2 c	butter or marg.	Cover over low heat 5 mins.
1 med	onion, chopped	
1 med	apple, chopped	
4 T	curry	

Optional additions: chopped mushrooms, celery, green pepper.

14 oz can	cream of mushroom soup	Add to onion, stir and heat. Pour over chicken and bake for 1 hr. at 350 degrees. Great served with rice and salad.
3/4 can	milk	
1 T	cornstarch	

The Wilson's, "JACONA", Vancouver, B.C.

CHICKEN "ITALIA"

1 lg	frying chicken, cut up	Arrange chicken pieces on foil lined shallow pan.

8 oz	bottled Italian dressing (any kind)	Shake well and pour over chicken. Bake for 1 hr. at 350 degrees.

Dodie Dayton, "VAGABUNDOS DEL MAR", Lodi, Ca.

La Grandeur's "Glory" — Gibsons.

B B Q

One mention of the word barbeque conjures up images of sunny afternoons spent outside with neighbours and friends dressed in deck shoes and shorts holding tall glasses of tea while succulent aromas waft from the grill. But where does it come from, this word "Barbeque"?

Texans assert that barbeques belong to them. "Hang a steer from a stout tree limb and build a fire to cook it then and there", says one source. The French say the word is theirs, an adaptation of the Creole expression, "de la barbe a la queue", meaning "from the beard to the tail", which illustrates the manner in which pirates who sailed the Maine roasted goats over open fires!

As pirates feasted on barbequed goat and Texans on barbequed steers, Captain George Vancouver barbequed salmon when he landed at Bonniebrook, British Columbia, on June 16, 1792. Speculation has it that Captian Vancouver was introduced to barbequing when he dined with Valdes and Galiano, the Spanish captains of the "SUTIL" and "MEXICANA" at Spanish Banks in June 1792, thus perfecting Vancouver's skills as they sailed together to Desolation Sound for the summer.

UP ON BARBEQUING

Here's what to expect from your barbeque. Barbequing imparts a distinctive flavour that can't be achieved under the broiler or in the skillet. The barbequed flavour is produced by juices from the food dripping on the hot coals and being vapourized back to the underside of the meat. At the same time the bottom surface is sealed by the heat to retain the juices.

Since it is the right "hot" surface and not the flame, whether gas or coal, that contributes most to developing the barbeque flavour, temperature and timing are prime factors.

TEMPERATURE

The trick is to catch the coals at the proper moment. When the coals have a thin coating of white ash and glow red the temperature is the hottest. Quick foods like steak and hamburger should be seared on high temperatures. As the ash increases, heat moderates to medium, suitable for fish, and low for poultry. To increase heat, tap coals to remove ash and move them closer together. To lower heat spread coals apart. When using either coal or gas barbeques, opening or closing the lid lowers or raises the temperature. Barbequing is a dry cooking process so when cooking beef or pork use high grill temperature to sear and seal flavourful juices, then reduce heat and cook to taste.

TIMING

Choose foods that will be cooked and ready at the same time or pre-cook "slower" foods by starting them sooner. A quick zap in a microwave, for example, is ideal for pre-cooking boned chicken parts. Onions and peppers partially cooked on the stovetop makes them easier to skewer and adjust their timing to, say, tomatoes and cubed meats.

Cooking time varies with type of food and thickness. A boned leg of lamb on a rotisserie takes over an hour whereas one inch cubes of lamb on a skewer take only ten minutes or so. Chicken breasts with bone in take 20 minutes but only eight minutes when de-boned. Pork should be well cooked. Make a small cut in the meat to see if it is ready. The pork should be white and moist and juices should run clear.

MORE ON BARBEQUING

Fish should be cooked carefully. Ten minutes for every inch of thickness is the general rule. Take care not to overcook. Leave skin on salmon fillets and barbeque skin-side down basting with a lemon juice/butter mixture. Cook only until beads of "milk" form on the surface — any further cooking will render the fish dry.

Selection of meats is a matter of personal taste, but low quality meat cannot be magically transformed into a top quality cut. A chuck steak won't be as palatable as a fillet, however with select marination chuck steak can be a very distinctive, flavourful cut. It is not easy to judge quality by the eye and even expensive cuts can be disappointing so ask your butcher for the meat aged and most suitable for your application. Usually tender cuts can be cooked quicker so better quality is desirable in barbequing.

BBQ TIPS

— Partially precook chicken pieces, hamburgers, etc. in a microwave if you have one available.

— Soak wooden shish kabob skewers in water.

— Brush oil on grill or use a non-stick spray to prevent sticking. Move meat one or two minutes after placing on grill.

— Use a tray made from foil to catch drippings from spit to avoid flare-ups. Fill with water for more tender meat.

— For a smoked flavour wrap a cupful of wood chips in foil, puncture with fork and place on "coals" for last half hour of closed lid barbequing.

— The easiest and most carefree roast to barbeque is a whole filet — sear all round and cook on grill over low to medium heat. When you think it is done, cross cut it in half and check for doneness on the inside. If it needs more cooking, sear cut sides and it will soon be ready — with a complete range of doneness too!

— Remember meat keeps cooking after it leaves the grill.

— Do not pierce meat either in preparation or cooking as this allows the juices to escape.

— Do not barbeque over fierce heat (except to seal) nor for that matter over too low a heat.

— After use soak grill overnight — it will be much easier to clean in the morning.

MARINATION

Whether for barbequing or other cooking method, the tenderizing effect on meats of wine and citrus juices is well known. The acid component breaks down the tissues and fibres and adds flavour in the process. Marinating inexpensive cuts of meat enhances their flavour and seals in moisture; finer cuts benefit by contact with wine, as well.

Marinate in glass, ceramic or plastic containers, turning the food at least once. A rule of thumb in timing is 6 hours at room temperature, 12 hours refrigerated. However, a little is better than none and 24 hours (refrigerated) would be an upper limit since the acids continue to break down the tissues once applied.

MARINATING TIPS

Use a tupperwear container to marinate meat or fish in. Leave it in the cooler and each time the cooler is opened, turn the container upside down.

Placing meats for marinating in plastic bag and adding the marinade is an effective way to obtain total immersion — just evacuate air and tie bag (place in bowl).

Another marination technique, just for sailors, is to put the container in the bilge and as you tack, the marinade moves to and fro.

If marination time is shortened, hold at room temperature rather than refrigerated (not in the sun, though).

Strain marinades into a screw top jar — they keep for weeks, refrigerated. Marinades with onions and vegies will keep about 5 days.

Use olive oil in cases where you wish a marinade coating of meats, e.g., whip olive oil and lime juice together to coat chicken pieces.

One method of tenderizing which is not as time sensitive is the softening technique — the immersion of beef in vegetable oil, with or without herbs and spcies, refrigerated for a minimum of 12 hours and up to days, is a favourite of mine.

Marinades with lemon or lime juice should be rinsed off before final preparation especially in sensitive foods such as fish.

Baste sparingly to avoid flareups when grilling. Heavy bodied bastes and those containing sugar or honey should be used only in the latter part of cooking. The chart on the following pages provides basic ingredients for marinating and basting as well as some examples of application.

THE A – B – Q's OF MARINATING

ACIDS	SPICES	HERBS	ADD FOR BASTER
Citrus		*Mild*	
Lemon	Cloves	Basil	Catsup
Lime	Cumin	Bay leaf	Miracle Whip
Orange	Curry	Marjoram	Tomato sauce
	Ginger	Parsley	Tomato paste
	Mustard (dry)		
Vinegars	Pepper		
		Medium	
White wine vinegar			Honey
Red wine vinegar	*Tangies*	Rosemary	Molasses
Cider vinegar		Savory	Sugar — white
	Onions	Tarragon	Sugar — brown
	Garlic	Thyme	
Wines and Spirits	Horseradish		
	Peppers	*Dominant*	
White wine	— serrano*		
Red wine	— mild	Oregano	
Whiskey	— jalapeno	Mint	
Sake	Soya sauce	Dill	
Sherry	Lemon rind		
Beer	Worchester sauce		
	Tabasco		
OILS			
Vegetable oil	*Remove seeds. Avoid		Note: Basters with sugar
Olive oil	contact with eyes and sen-		should only be used in final
	sitive skin.		minutes.

BUILD A MARINADE — EXAMPLE (Each makes approx. 1 cup)

BEEF

1/4 c white wine	2 cloves	2 t parsley	Add to marinade when
1/4 c white vinegar	1 small onion, chopped	1/4 t thyme	beef goes to grill:
1/4 c vegetable oil	1 clove garlic, chopped		1/4 c catsup
1/3 c whiskey	1 t mustard		
1/3 c vegetable oil	1 small onion, chopped		
	1/4 c soya sauce		
	pepper		

PORK

4 oz frozen orange juice conc.	1 t mustard		Combine with a portion
1/2 c water	1 T soya sauce		of marinade for baste:
1/3 c white wine vinegar	salt		1/4 c brown sugar
	pepper		3 T honey

LAMB

1/3 c lemon juice	1 t lemon rind, grated	1/2 t rosemary, crushed	
1/3 c vegetable oil	1 T worchester sauce		
	1 clove garlic, crushed		
	salt & pepper		
1/2 c vegetable oil	2 T worchester sauce	1 T mint	
1/4 c vinegar	salt		
	pepper		

CHICKEN

1/2 c olive oil	1 small onion, chopped		
1/4 c lime juice	1 clove garlic, chopped		
1/4 c vegetable oil	1 small onion, chopped	1/4 t marjoram	Combine and simmer 10 mins.
1/4 c white vinegar	1/4 t worchester sauce	1/4 t basil	a portion of marinade
1/4 c	1/4 t black pepper		for baste:
			1 small can tomato paste
			2 T brown sugar
			1/4 c water

FISH

1/2 c beer	2 T worchester sauce	1 t parsley	
3 T lemon juice	1 t lemon rind, grated		
1/2 c olive oil	1/4 t black pepper		

TORTUGA SALMON BBQ

$2/3$ c	**Miracle Whip**
$1/3$ c	**melted butter**
1 T	**liquid honey**
1 T	**wine vinegar**
$1/2$ t	**dill, chopped**
1 t	**lemon juice**

Mix till smoth and brush on both sides of salmon fillets.

Grill till sauce browns, turn fish over, coat top with more sauce and cook till top glazes. Serve with more sauce on side.

Joe says this recipe is so good he carries it around in his wallet so it will be ever handy!

Joe Holmes, "TORTUGA BAY", Thormanby Island, B.C.

SHIO YAKI

salmon, rockcod, red snapper, herring, etc. (not dogfish)

Scale, clean and fillet. Lay flesh side down on paper towels and sprinkle skin liberally with salt (coarse recommended). Hold overnight cool.

Rinse off salt, pat dry, grill 10 mins. per inch turning once. Skin should be crisp and slightly brown. Or bake in 450 degree oven for same length of time. Enjoy hot or cold! Tanoshiko!!

Brian Stanhope, "BILLY'S DREAM", N. Vancouver, B.C.

KWAKUITL BBQ CLAMS

SERVES 4

4 doz   butter clams

Boil in water till shells open, reserve water.

Remove meat from shells, rinse in reserved water which will be used also for basting. Thread on thin cedar sticks (presoaked in water). Bbq slowly till nice and brown, baste often.

As stated by Henry Speck, famous for his Indian carvings.

Henry Speck, "HIMANIS, GWA-WAS", Hopetown, B.C.

FOILED VEGIES — BBQ

Place your desired portions on double heavy duty foil, season with salt and pepper, add a favourite herb, a little butter and water per serving, wrap loosely and double seal edges.

Timetable in Minutes

Asparagus	10/20	Cauliflower	15/20
Beans	25/35	Sweet Corn	20/25
Broccoli	10/15	Mushrooms	8/13
Carrots (sliced)	30/40	Peas	15/20
Leeks	30/40	Zucchini (sliced)	25/30

CARROTS — *1 Serving*

1 c	carrots, sliced
1 T	butter
1 T	dry sherry (opt.)
$1/2$ t	tarragon
to taste	salt and pepper

Wrap in foil and grill 30-40 mins.

Variation: Carrots and Leeks — prepare as above.

MEXICAN CORN — *4 Servings*

$1^1/2$ c	corn (4 cobs)
3 T	butter
$1/3$ c	onion, chopped
$1/3$ c	gr. pepper, chopped
2	tomatoes, chopped
$1/4$ t	oregano
to taste	salt and pepper

Remove kernels from corn cobs, place with other ingredients on buttered foil. Seal and grill 15 mins. one side, turn and cook 10 mins. on other.

CARAMELIZED CORN — *1 Serving*

1	corn cob
2 T	butter
1 t	brown sugar

Remove husk and silk from corn, place on foil, brush with butter, sprinkle with sugar, wrap and seal. Grill 20 mins. turning occasionally.

MORE FOILED FAVOURITES

ONION BAKE — *1 Serving*

1 med	onion
1 T	butter
1/2 t	sugar
to taste	salt and pepper

Make two cuts in top of onion, add butter, etc. Wrap in foil, grill close to coals 40-50 mins.

SMOTHERED ONIONS — *4 Servings*

2 T	butter
4	onions, sliced
1 t	Worcester sauce
dash	tabasco sauce
to taste	salt and pepper

Lay thinly sliced onions and seasonings on buttered foil. Seal and grill 20 mins., turn and grill 15 mins. longer.

SHERRIED MUSHROOMS — *4 Servings*

1 lb	mushrooms
1/4 c	butter
2 T	dry sherry
1 t	coriander
to taste	salt and pepper

Slice mushrooms 1/4" thick and place on foil, sprinkle with seasoning, add butter and sherry, seal and grill 10 mins. Garnish with parsley.

BBQ BANANAS SPICED — *4 Servings*

6	bananas, peeled
2 T	lemon juice
2 T	brown sugar
2 T	butter
	cinnamon or nutmeg

Cut bananas in pieces, lay on foil, brush with juice, sprinkle with sugar, dot with butter, dash with cinnamon.

Lay in coals for 5 mins or on grill, turning, for longer.

POTATOES — *1 Serving*

1 med	potato, peeled and 1″ sliced
1 med	onion, ¹/₂″ sliced
1 T	butter

Alternate potato and onion layers on foil, moisten with butter, wrap tightly, grill 20 mins. one side then 15 mins. on other.

GERMAN POTATOES — *4 Servings*

4 med	potatoes
1 c	onions, chopped
¹/₂ c	gr. pepper, chopped
¹/₄ c	butter
¹/₄ t	caraway seed (opt.)
to taste	salt and pepper

Pare and cut potatoes into ¹/₂″ cubes. Place on foil, add rest of ingredients. Grill 20 mins., turn and grill 20 mins. more. Toss and serve.

POTATO — *1 Serving*

1 med	potato
2 T	butter
2 T	dry onion soup mix

Cut "V" slot almost through potato, fill with butter and soup mix. Wrap in foil, grill 1 hr.

POTATO — *1 Serving*

1 med	potato
1 T	butter
2 t	parmesan cheese
1 t	grated onion
to taste	celery salt and pepper

Quarter potato and trim to form sticks. Lay on foil, top with other ingredients, grill 30 mins.

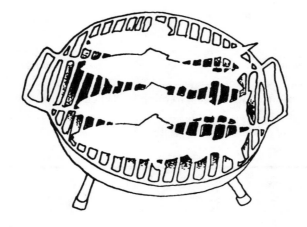

GREEK KABOBS

SERVES 4

2 lb	pork shoulder	Cut pork into 1¹/₂″ cubes and put into large bowl.
1 lge	onion, grated	Combine all ingredients and pour
1	gr. pepper, grated	over pork. Toss to fully coat. If using
2 T	vegetable oil	whole lemons, chop and include the
6 T	lemon juice or	peel. Marinate for a few hours,
	juice of 3 lemons	retoss, then thread on bamboo
4 T	red wine	skewers so they just touch. Lay in
¹/₂ t	oregano	shallow bowl, pour juices over and
¹/₂ t ea.	salt and pepper	marinate for few hours more.

Cook over medium coals till brown and cooked through.

Cathy Fouchard, "CANTYRE", Prince George, B.C.

BEEF KABOBS

2 lb	beef sirloin	Cut beef into 1¹/₄″ cubes and put into large bowl.
¹/₂ c	red wine	Combine all ingredients and pour
¹/₂ c	vegetable oil	over beef. Toss to fully coat.
1 clove	garlic, diced	Marinate for at least 2 hours.
2 T	ketchup	
1 T	vinegar	
1 t	Worcester sauce	
1 t	sugar	
¹/₂ t ea.	marjoram and rosemary	
¹/₂ t	salt	
	mushrooms	Alternate on skewers with beef.

Cook over medium coals, turning frequently, till beef is done to your taste.

Diane Anderson, "MAQUINNA PT.", Gibsons, B.C.

PORK RIBS

3 lbs	country style pork ribs	Wrap in heavy foil and place on bbq for 40 mins., turning once.
$^1/_3$ c	marmalade	Heat together in small saucepan.
$^1/_4$ c	lemon juice	
$^1/_4$ c	soya sauce	
1 clove	garlic, minced	
2 T	cornstarch	Mix, add to above and cook stirring
2 T	water	till thickened.

Remove foil packet from grill, dip ribs in sauce and cook, basting and turning, for 5 mins.

David Pethick, "MISKA", Gibsons, B.C.

BEEF RIBS

2 T	butter	Saute in butter till soft.
1 stalk	celery, grated	
1	carrot, grated	
1	onion, chopped	
1 clove	garlic, minced	
1 c	tomato sauce	Add to above, simmer 30 mins. and
$^1/_4$ c	cider vinegar	strain.
$^1/_4$ c	brown sugar	
3 T	Worcester sauce	
4 lbs	lean beef ribs	Simmer bones in sauce 30 mins., turn, cook till tender, remove from pot, sprinkle with pepper and celery salt and grill, basting for 15-20 mins.
to taste	pepper and celery salt	

Can also be used for cooked bones from a roast.

Andy Katz, "JEREMIAH 87", Vancouver, B.C.

A WHOLE CHICKEN

SERVES 4

Take a $2^1/_2$ — $3^1/_2$ lb chicken — cut along each side of backbone with boning knife — remove backbone and neck, spread apart and pop breast bone. Remove cartilage and cut off wing tipes. Lay out flat and bash chicken flat with fish bonker or side of cleaver.

$^1/_4$ c	vegetable oil	Saute onion till soft.
$^1/_2$ c	onion, chopped	
4 oz tin	green chilis, chopped, or picante chili sauce	Add and heat. Add chicken, breast side up, simmer 6 mins., puncture skin, turn and simmer 6 mins. more.
$^1/_2$ c	wine	
$^1/_4$ c	peanut butter	
1 T	cumin	

Drain chicken, reserving sauce. Place whole chicken on bbq. skin side up. Brown, turn, brown other side. Mix remaining sauce with rice. Serve with side salad.

Kim McGinnis, "MAUREEN", Gibsons, B.C.

FOILED FISH DINNER

SERVES 4

$^1/_4$ c	butter or marg.	Combine and place 1 T mixture on each of 4 pieces of foil.
2 T	lemon juice	
1 T	dill	
$1^1/_2$ c	potatoes, fine cubed	Divide potatoes and carrots equally on buttered foil, top with slice of onion.
1 c	carrots, julienned	
4 slices	onion	
$1^1/_2$ lb	fish fillets	Cut into 4, place on top of onion slices, top with remaining butter mixture.
4 slices	processed cheese	Place a slice of cheese on top of each package, seal tightly and bbq over hot coals 30 mins.

Tiny Clark, "C-LARK", Square Bay, B.C.

ERNIE'S PORK ROAST

SERVES 6

Ernie insists this bbq technique produces the most moist and tasty roast you have ever eaten. Place a shallow pan of water under the roast — collected juices from the roast together with the remaining water forms the basis for your sauce.

3 lb	pork loin roast	Rub with salt and pepper. Roast
to taste	pepper and Lawry's salt	covered on rotisserie or fat side up on heated grill to 170 degrees, 1½-2 hrs.

Peach Sauce		Chop and mash or blend on med.
15 oz		speed till smoth. Use ½ mixture to
can	peaches, drained	baste roast during last ½ hr. of
3 T	brown sugar	cooking, reserving other half.
1 T	ketchup	
½ T	vinegar	
2 t	salt	
1 t	vegetable oil	
½ t	ground ginger	

When roast is done remove and let set 15 mins. Meanwhile add drippings to reserved baste, heat and serve on the side.

Ernie Shorthouse, "SEASCAPE", Ashcroft, B.C.

OYSTERS KILPATRICK

To 'tide you over' while the roast is cooking!

2 slices	bacon, chopped	Saute and crumble.

1 doz	oysters	Remove top shell and arrange on
to taste	Worcester sauce, salt and pepper	ovenwear or grill. Season to taste and top with bacon.

Broil, bbq, or bake till heated through.

Wendy Laskmann, "QUEST", Burnaby, B.C.

"Miska" & young sailors — (Recipes 112, 113, 140).

Q
U
I
K

ISLAND ODYSSEY '86

Between May 29 and June 28, 1986, the Island Odyssey travelled from Victoria, up the east coast of Vancouver Island and south on the west coast back to Victoria, reliving the adventures of Capt. George Vancouver through the Inside Passage and visiting Nootka and other west coast harbours.

The "SPIRIT OF CHEMAINUS", launched September 14, 1985, is a sailing replica of the "CADBORO", which first entered Victoria Harbour in 1837. The "SPIRIT" accompanied the Odyssey flotilla in its first week through Discovery Passage and Broughton Straits to Port Hardy. It thereupon returned to Chemainus to carry sight-seeing Expo 86 visitors at its name town on Vancouver Island — home of the "Festival of Murals".

Of the 53 starting boats who circumnavigated Vancouver Island were Dr. A. B. Craddock's "THE TESILYA", of Sidney, B.C. and David Raymond's "KALYNDA J." of Yakima, Wa. The following pages contain recipes for some of the food served on these three boats during their participation in "The Island Odyssey".

Mary Waller, a first time chef in a serious sailing situation assumed her role on "THE TESILYA". Mary, up to the challenge, assembled an impressive dossier for the impending task ahead! The following is an extract:

COSMOPOLITAN HOT DOGS

The basics are processed meats in various taste styles from regular to smokies and European; and buns, which can be traditional, plain or with sesame seed topping; rye, pita or Vienna bread; thin pancakes, croissants, tortillas or bagels — you name it — your wrapper is the basis of bewitching hot dogs!

NOW TOP IT

CANADIAN
Cook and crumble bacon, mix with grated cheddar, spread over hot dog in bun, broil.

TEXAN
Top with chili, sprinkle with grated cheese.

SWISS
Wrap hot dog with slice of Swiss cheese, place in bun, top with sauerkraut, broil to melt cheese.

GERMAN
Heat sauerkraut with caraway seed, add chopped dill pickle and sugar.

ORIENTAL
Mix Chinese mustard and sweet and sour sauce, spread over hot dog, add crisp noodles.

AMERICAN
Top with shredded lettuce, chopped gr. onions, celery, tomatoes, drizzle with favourite salad dressing.

MEXICAN
Spread with hot salsa sauce.

GREEK
Spread with chopped olives, sour cream or onion dip.

HAWAIIAN
Combine chopped green pepper, pineapple and sweet and sour sauce.

ITALIAN
Spread on pizza sauce, top with grated mozarella cheese. Broil.

Mary Waller, "TESILYA", Sidney, B.C.

. . . More Island Odessey opposite.

SPIRIT OF CHEMAINUS BRAN MUFFINS — SERVES 12

1/2 c	margarine	Cream together.
3/4 c	brown sugar	
3 T	molasses	Mix together and add to above.
1 1/2 c	bran	
1 t	baking powder	
1 1/4 c	flour, sifted	
	dried fruits, such as raisins, dates, apricots, etc.	Chop any fruits that are large and add to above.
1 t	baking soda	Stir soda into milk, quickly add to dry ingredients then fold in egg.
1 c	sour milk	
1	egg, beaten	

Bake in muffin tins at 375-400 degrees for 15 min.

Jennifer Spicer, "THE SPIRIT OF CHEMAINUS", Chemainus, B.C.

CABBAGE PATCH SOUP — SERVES 4

Amount	Ingredient	Instruction
1 lb	ground beef	Crumble and cook, pour off fat.
25 oz can	crushed tomatoes	Combine with beef and simmer 45 mins. or longer.
5 c	water	
15 oz can	kidney beans	
1/4 c	celery, chopped	
1 pkg	taco seasoning	
1 med	head of cabbage, shredded	Add and continue cooking 1/2 hr. Top with grated cheddar cheese.

Lynn Raymond, "KALYNDA J." Yakima, Wa.

TOMATO RICE

1 can	soup	Bring to boil over med. heat.
2 c	water	
1 t	basil	
1 c	rice, uncooked	Add, reduce heat and simmer 25 mins.

FISH CREOLE

1 can	soup	Stir and heat.
1/4 c	water	
2 c	fish in bite size pieces	Add, cover and simmer till fish is cooked, about 10 mins.
1	gr. pepper, chopped	
1 clove	garlic, crushed	
1 t	thyme	

CURRIED CHICKEN

4	chicken breasts	Brown breasts in butter.
1 T	butter	
1 can	soup	Combine and add to chicken, cover and simmer 10 mins. each side.
1/4 c	water	
1 1/2 t	curry	

Judy Preston, "YELLOW BIRD", Halfmoon Bay, B.C.

ITALIAN SAUSAGE, BEAN AND POTATO STEW

6 (1 lb)	Italian sausages	Brown sausages and push to one
1 lg	onion, sliced	side. Saute onion and garlic tender.
1 clove	garlic, minced	Add green pepper, saute 2 mins.
1	gr. pepper, sliced	longer. Stir in potatoes, sauce and
2 lg	potatoes, diced	seasonings. Cover, simmer till
8 oz		potatoes are tender.
can	tomato sauce	
1 t	basil	
	salt and pepper	

16 oz		Add to above and heat.
can	kidney beans, drained	

REUBEN NOODLES ROMANOFF

5.5 oz		Prepare noodles to package
pkg	Noodles Romanoff	directions — increase milk to $^1/_2$ c.
$^1/_2$ t	caraway seeds (optional)	Stir in caraway seed.

$^1/_2$ lb	chopped corned beef	Stir in corned beef, cheese and
2-3		sauerkraut; heat through. Can be
slices	Swiss cheese, diced	layered $^1/_2$ noodles, beef, cheese,
8 oz		kraut, other $^1/_2$ noodles and baked
can	sauerkraut, drained	25 mins. at 350.

SALMON ROMANOFF

6 oz		Prepare according to package
pkg	noodles w/Cheddar cheese and sour cream sauce	directions.

8 oz	salmon, canned or fresh	Add to above and heat.
4 oz		
can	mushrooms, drained	
1 c	cottage cheese	
3 T	gr. onion, chopped	
$^1/_4$ t	dill weed	

MILLTOWN SAILING ASSOCIATION, Everett, Wa.

PRESSURE COOKING MAGIC

There is GALLEY MAGIC when Anne Strench of "BODARIS" whips out her 6 qt "Sensor" pressure cooker for, to her, pressure cookers were made for boats and should be standard equipment on all cruising yachts. They are fast, versatile and economical. The use of pressure cookers reduces the heat buildup in the galley due to cooking time reduction; and the time saved can better be applied to relaxing on a hot summer day. As a cooking technique, pressure cooking tenderizes cheaper cuts of meat; as well, the high temperature cooking is practical for any older meats on board. For a one-pot casserole a pressure cooker excels and most of your oven casseroles can be cooked in one quarter of the time. For fish, put a covered dish in the cooker to maintain the delicate flavour. There is an infinite variety of applications for a pressure cooker — it doubles as an unpressurized pot and is also a slow cooker — truly versatile.

MANHATTAN CLAM CHOWDER   SERVES 4

4 slices	bacon, diced	Brown in cooker.
$^2/_3$ c	onion, sliced	Saute with bacon, drain fat.
2 c	potatoes, cubed	Place in cooker, close and cook
2	carrots, diced	pressurized for 5 mins. Let pressure
28 oz		drop slowly.
can	tomatoes, whole	
1 stalk	celery, chopped	
$^1/_3$ c	gr. pepper, chopped	
$^1/_4$ t	pepper	
1 t	salt	
1 t	thyme	
2 c	water	
	liquid from canned clams	
2-8 oz		Add and simmer 5 mins. without lid.
cans	clams	
1 c	water	
1 T	parsley	

HARD COOKED EGGS

10-12	eggs	Place in pressure cooker on cooking
1 c	water	rack, close cover and pressure cook 6 mins. Cool cooker all at once.

. . . More P.C. Magic opposite.

CARROTS & PINEAPPLE   SERVES 4

2 lb	carrots, sliced	Place in cooker, close and pressure
2 T	butter	cook 3 mins. Cool cooker.

13 oz		Drain, add, heat thru and serve.
can	pineapple chunks	

STEAK AND RICE

1¹/₂ lb	round steak	Cube meat and brown in cooker.
2 T	vegetable oil	

¹/₃ c	onion, chopped	Add and cook at 15 lb preesure for
¹/₃ c	celery, chopped	10 mins. Cool cooker all at once.
¹/₄ c	tomato sauce	Serve with rice.
¹/₂ c	mushrooms	
²/₃ c	sour cream	
2 t	Worcester sauce	
¹/₂ t	salt	

STEAMED CLAMS

	live clams	Wash and soak overnight in water
	coarse salt	with oatmeal or cornmeal added.
2 c	water	Place clams on rack in cooker,
		sprinkle with coarse salt. Close and
		pressure cook 2-3 mins. Cool
		cooker quickly. Serve clam liquor in
		separate dish.

POPCORN

¹/₃ c	vegetable oil	Place in cooker, close but do not
¹/₂ c	popping corn	pressurize — heat. When popping
		stops, pour into bowl, drizzle with salt
		and butter.

Anne Strench, "BODARIS", North Vancouver, B.C.

QUIK & EASY MEXCIAN CASSEROLE

SERVES 8-10

16 oz can	whole kernel corn	Drain corn, mix with other ingredients.
15 oz can	chili beans	
4 oz can	green chili salsa	
2 c	sour cream	In a 2 qt casserole layer $1/2$ of mixture, sour cream, corn chips, cheese, repeat layers. Bake at 350 degrees for 20 mins.
1 med pgk	Frito's corn chips	
2 c	cheddar cheese, shredded	

Julie Jones, "ARCADIA", Newport Beach, Ca.

HOT CRAB & AVOCADO SALAD

SERVES 8

1 c	crab meat	Mix together.
$1/2$ c	celery, chopped	
2	hard-cooked eggs, chopped	
$1/2$ c	mayonnaise	
1 t	onion, chopped	
4	ripe avocado	Cut unpeeled avocados in half, remove pit, brush with lemon juice, fill with crab mix. Sprinkle with bread crumbs and salt, drizzle with butter. Bake at 400 degrees for 10 mins.
$1/4$ c	bread crumbs	
1 T	melted butter	
	lemon juice	
	salt	

Claire Rainer, "BLUE SKY NO. 1", Hopkins Landing, B.C.

126

HOT "ALLCAN"

10 oz can	cream of chicken, mushroom or celery soup	Heat undiluted.
6 oz can	chicken chunks, turkey or tuna	Add, juice and all.
	dry onion celery, chopped	Add.
1 pkg	Ramon noodles	Add, broken up (not seasoning pkg).

Watch carefully. If dry, add a touch of water — simmer about 5 ins. Serve with salad.

Betty Marsh, "S/V KINGWNEQ", Vancouver, B.C.

ZIPPY FISH

1 lb	fish fillets, cod, halibut, sole	Place in single layer in greased baking dish.
¹/₄ c 2 t 2 T	mayonnaise hot English mustard onion, finely chopped paprika	Combine, spread over fish, sprinkle with paprika.

Bake in 450 degree oven for 10 mins. — a little longer if fillets are thick.

Jennie Ambrose, "M/V CHANGI", W. Vancouver, B.C.

127

SALMON HURRY-CURRY

1/4 c	onion, chopped	Saute in med. sauce pan.
1 T	butter or marg.	

8 oz can	salmon or leftover salmon	Break into chunks and add.

10 oz can	cream of celery soup	Add, stir to blend. Bring to boil, reduce heat, cover and simmer 5-10 mins.
1 t	curry powder	
1/4 t	ginger	
	salt and pepper	

Serve on cooked rice with your favourite condiments: chutney, chopped hard boiled egg, raisins, diced tomato, etc.

Jim McKay, "COLLEEN", Vancouver, B.C.

THE KOH CASSEROLE BASE

1 box	Liptons mornay casserole base	Make as directed except use wine for liquid. Add mushrooms with their liquid.
1/2-3/4 c	dry white wine	
10 oz can	mushrooms	

This is great for boaters. Use for celery, water chestnuts, shrimp, salmon, crab, etc.

Pat Kayll, "THE KOH", W. Vancouver, B.C.

The charm of fishing is that it is the pursuit of what is elusive but attainable, a perpetual series of occasions for hope.

JOHN BUCHAN

LIVER JULIENNE

1 lb	**liver**	Cut into 2¹/₂″ × ¹/₄″ strips.
1 **¹/₄ c**	**egg** **bouillon, double strength**	Beat together, pour into shallow pan with liver. Let stand 3 mins, turn and let stand 3 mins. more.

Pour all into preheated non-stick pan and cook over moderate heat 3 min., turn and cook 3 mins. more.

Maureen Naseth, "SCHATZI", Gibsons, B.C.

EASY CLAM CHOWDER

4 slices	**bacon, cooked and crumbled**	Fry bacon until crisp, pour off fat and set on one side.
2 T **1 c** **2 cans** **2 cans** **2 soup** **cans**	**butter** **onion, chopped** **minced clams** **cream of potato soup** **milk**	Saute onion in butter, add drained clams, potato soup, milk and crumbled bacon. Heat slowly, simmer 3 mins.

Dodie Dayton, "VAGABUNDOS DEL MAR", Lodi, Ca.

"The Arcadia" (story p. 164).

THE "TAI-JOHN" TALE

Leila Hanson was the chef for the skeleton crew on board the "TAI-JOHN", when the towline was dropped in international waters May 1982. The "TAI-JOHN" started her engine and began a 6,300 mile, 19-day voyage from Vancouver to Taiwan with soaring albatross for company. Some months earlier the "TAI-JOHN" had been severely beaten in a storm while off Midway and had limped into Vancouver, B.C. beyond repair.

The tired old 500 foot freighter was patched up for the journey to the scrapyard. She left Vancouver under the tow of the 1912 vintage tug, "ISLAND COMMANDER". This was not an unusual trip, towing and dropping a ship at sea. In earlier days the "ISLAND COMMANDER'S" first role had been to tow sailing ships clear of the coast.

And so a tale evolved on the high seas and Leila was a part of it!! (see recipe page 133).

DO-AHEAD

NEW YEAR'S PLUM PUDDING

As Vancouver's expedition entered the new year of 1793, all hands were served plum pudding with rum (a tot that is). Whether on a "frost-bite" cruise or at home, plum pudding is a satisfying finishing touch to your New Year's dinner — with rum, of course!!

1/2 c	seedless raisins	Chop fruits lightly, add rum and let
1/4 c	candied orange and lemon peel	stand several hours.
1/4 c	citron, diced	
1/4 c	candied cherries	
3 oz	rum	

1/2 c	butter or marg.	Combine in order given then add
1 c	fine bread crumbs	dried fruits and mix well. Pour into
6 T	sugar	ring mold or bowl and cover tightly.
1/4 c	flour	
1/4 t ea	salt and cloves	
1/2 t ea	cinnamon and nutmeg	
1/4 c	almonds, chopped	
3	eggs, well beaten	

Set mold on rack in large pot. Pour boiling water around it to come well up sides of mold. Cover pot and boil for 6 hrs. adding water as needed. Serve at once or cool, refrigerate and re-steam for 1 hr. aboard.

CREAMY WINE SAUCE

1.2 c	honey or light corn syrup	Heat together.
6 T	light cream	

1 T	margarine	Blend and add, cook stirring.
2 t	flour	

1	egg yolk, beaten	Stir in and cook 1 min.

2 T	sherry	Add and serve.

Diana Gray, "FANTASY", Vancouver, B.C.

SCALLOPED PINEAPPLE

SERVES 4

1/2 c	sugar	Mix together and add 1 c of juice
1/2 c	flour	from pineapple below. Mix till smoth, set aside.

26 oz can	pineapple, cubed	Layer alternately, cover with mix above.
1 1/2 c	cheddar cheese, grated	

Bake at 350 degrees for 45 mins. Serve with chicken or ham.

Edith Thorsness, "LEILANI", Vernon, B.C.

TAI-JOHN CURRIED PICKLED FISH

SERVES 9-12

4 lg	onions	Boil in large pot for 10 mins.
12	whole peppercorns	
6	whole bay leaves	
4 c	water	

3 T	curry powder	Mix dry ingredients in a bowl, slowly
2 T	cornstarch	blend in vinegar then add mix into
3 T	sugar	boiling onions, stirring constantly.
2 1/2 c	vinegar	Add raisins.
4 T	raisins	

4 lbs	cod fillets, fresh or frozen	Thaw (if frozen) and season cod. Dip
	salt and pepper	each piece in milk then flour. Fry in
	milk and flour	hot oil in skillet.

Remove fish to large warmed casserole, keep warm while pouring curry sauce over. Cover casserole, refrigerate 2 days before eating. Serve hot or cold.

Leila Hanson, San Francisco, Ca., "TAI-JOHN"

ART'S PICKLED ORANGE PRAWNS

4 lbs	raw prawns, in shell	Slightly undercook in boiling, dilled,
6	dill sprigs	salted water, say 1 – 1^1/$_2$ mins. Peel, drain and dry.
1 lg	onion, sliced	Place shrimp in bowl with onion
2	oranges, sliced	rings, orange, ginger root and
1 piece	ginger root, sliced	parsley, toss. Transfer to sterilized
^{1}/$_4$ c	parsley, chopped	wide mouth jars by packing in
1 ea.	bay leaf and dill sprig (per jar)	alternate layers. Add bay leaf and dill.
2 c	cider vinegar	Combine ingredients and bring to
^{1}/$_3$ c ea.	olive and vegetable oils	boil. Pour over packed jars slowly so as to flow to the bottom. Seal. Chill
2 t	salt	at least 48 hrs. before serving. Keeps
^{1}/$_2$ t	dry mustard	for weeks refrigerated but will not last
^{1}/$_4$ t	ground mace	that long!!
2 T	pickling spice	

Art McGinnis, "GIBSONS MARINA", Gibsons, B.C.

SWEETPEA SALAD

spinach, fresh	Layer in glass or clear plastic bowl.
eggs, hard boiled	Layers should be quite thick.
red onions, sliced	
shrimp or turkey/ chicken chunks	
frozen peas, thawed	
lettuce, shredded	
sour cream	Mix in equal parts. Frost at least 1"
mayonnaise	thick. Do not toss.
cheese, shredded	Top generously. Refrigerate
bacon bits	overnight.

"THE SWEETPEA" is an 18' electric Bay Boat for harbour cruising.

Julie Jones, "THE SWEETPEA", Balboa Bay, Ca.

International food writer, Arthur Schwartz, says, "Caesar Cardini, who owned a small restaurant in Tijuana in 1920 (long after Capt. George Vancouver passed by), invented a salad and named it after himself. As it happened, Caesar ran out of food. All that was left in his kitchen were crates of romaine lettuce, eggs, romano cheese, oil and lemons. In a moment of inspiration (so says Schwartz), Cardini, who had been a salad man in his earlier days, assembled his staff, his carts and salad bowls, pepper mills and graters, and in a showy performance presented what he had with fanfare." To Caesar, this is Hayden's version.

Prepare the gutsy dressing shoreside for later cozy cove dining.

2 heads	**romaine lettuce**	Wash, break, spin or pat dry, store in plastic bag
4 slices	**bread**	Cube into croutons and dry on cabin top on sunny day (or otherwise).
2 cloves **¹/₄** **1³/₄ oz** **²/₃ c**	**garlic** **lemon with peel** **anchovies** **olive oil**	Blend garlic, lemon and anchovies on high speed with half of the oil. When smooth, slowly add balance of oil.
2	**eggs**	Add and blend till creamy. Will keep 6 or 7 days refrigerated. Store in closed jar.

Pour dressing over lettuce, add croutons, parmesan cheese, salt and pepper and toss.

Hayden Killam, SECRET COVE MARINA, Secret Cove, B.C.

Hit the ball over the fence and you can take your time going around the bases.

JOHN WRAPER

HEARTY FISHERMAN'S DELIGHT | SERVES 4-6

Stan insists an old pot is essential for the experience and atmosphere in this hearty meal afloat or shoreside! And better next day too!

2 doz	clams	Steam and chop, set aside. Reserve liquor.
1 doz	scallops	Put all ingredients into your old pot
8 lg	cod fillet	together with reserved clam nectar,
4	carrots, chopped	adding water if necessary to make 1
4 stalks	celery, chopped	qt. Simmer 30 mins.
3	onions, sliced	
1 clove	garlic, minced	
2	lemon slices	
	salt and pepper	
3 lg	salmon fillets, steamed	Remove bones and skin. Add to above with reserved clams and simmer for a further 40 mins.
2	egg yolks	Beat yolks and cream, add dill.
1 c	cream	Blend into pot at last moment.
3 T	dill, chopped	

Stan Dixon, "MAC-KIN-JUTT", Sechelt, B.C.

QUICHE TARTS | MAKES 4 DOZEN

Line four dozen tart pans with pastry. Sprinkle uncooked shells with any combination of cooked bacon, ham, shrimp, crab, chopped green onions, mushrooms or anything else your imagination can come up with. Top with grated mozarella cheese.

6	eggs, beaten	Beat eggs slightly, combine with
$1^1/_4$ c	whipping cream	other ingredients, pour over filling —
$^1/_2$ c	milk	do not overflow. Bake at 400
$^1/_2$ t	salt	degrees for 25 mins. Avoid the last
1 t	dillweed	minute rush — freeze and reheat
2 shakes	cayenne	aboard.

Dot Gibson, "S/B MALIS", Tofino, B.C.

CHILI CON CARNE "ADRIENNE"

SERVES 8

2 lbs	top round steak, cubed	Brown in 4 T oil in heavy skillet, drain, transfer to 4 qt pot.
6 T	vegetable oil	
2 c	onion, chopped	Add 2 T oil to skillet and cook
2 T	garlic, chopped	vegetables 4–5 mins., stirring.
1 c	gr. pepper, chopped	Remove from heat.
4 T	chili powder	Add to skillet and stir well.
1 t ea.	salt and oregano	
1 t	red pepper flakes or pinch cayenne	
$^1/_2$ t ea.	sweet basil and sugar	
$^1/_4$ t ea.	paprika and black pepper	
6 oz can	tomato paste	Add to skillet, stir, then add to meat. Bring to boil, lower heat and simmer $1-1^1/_4$ hrs, stirring occasionally.
10 oz can	beef bouillon, no water	
1 c	red wine	
6 med	tomatoes, peeled and crushed or	
19 oz can	tomatoes	
$1^1/_2$ c	dark red kidney beans	Drain beans, add to chili with pepperoni, cook 15–20 mins. longer.
1 c	pepperoni sticks, chopped	

Make ahead and refrigerate for 2nd night out or freeze in plastic container for later use.

Ian Glen, "THE ADRIENNE", Selma Park, B.C.

Why do we love the sea? It is because it has some potent power to make us think things we like to think.

ROBERT HENRI

CHINESE BEEF & RICE CASSEROLE

SERVES 4

1 c	long grain rice	Pour into 2 qt casserole.
2 c	boiling water	
1 t	salt	
1 lg	onion, chopped	Saute vegetables until soft, stir in
1 c	celery, diced	beef, cook until it has lost rawness,
2 T	butter	add to rice in casserole.
1 lb	ground beef	
	sugar	Stir into casserole, bake covered 1¼
1/3 c	soy sauce	hrs. at 350 degrees.
4 oz can	mushrooms, drained	
1/2 c	cashews	Add, cook uncovered further 15 mins. This freezes well.

Marion Brant, "FOUR WINDS", Sechelt, B.C.

DO AHEAD POTATOES

SERVES 4

3 lg	potatoes	Cook, boiling till tender. Drain and mash well.
1/3 c	cream cheese, soft	Add and beat in till fluffy.
1/4 c	sour cream	
2 T	butter	
1	egg, beaten	
2 t	salt	
dash	pepper	

Cool slightly and spread in greased casserole, dot with more butter, refrigerate. To serve, remove from refrigerator 1 hr. before serving, place for 30 mins. in 350 degree oven or till heated through. Will keep for 4-5 days refrigerated.

A DOG'S BISCUIT

While preparing your do-ahead dishes, why not whip up a batch of these treats for your favourite on-board pet.

2 c	whole wheat flour	Mix together.
$1/4$ c	cornmeal	
$1/2$ c	soy flour	
1 t	bone meal	
1 t	sea salt	
$1/4$ c	sunflower seeds	
2 T	oil, melted butter or fat	Mix together and add to dry ingredients. Knead for a few mins.,
$1/4$ c	blackstrap molasses	let rest $1/2$ hr., roll to $1/2$ in. thickness.
2	eggs	Cut into shapes, bake on greased
$1/4$ c	milk	cookie sheet 30 mins. at 350 degrees. Leave in oven with heat turned off for 1 hr. or more.

David Pethick, "MISKA", Gibsons, B.C.

THE CAT'S MEOW

Your cat (and even your dog) will love these special biscuits.

1 c	whole wheat or rye flour	Mix together.
$1/4$ c	soy flour	
$1/2$ t	bone meal	
3 T	oil or lard	Mix together, add to dry ingredients
$1/3$ c	hot water	and mix well. Roll out on cookie sheet, cut into small squares or ribbons and bake till golden at 350 degrees.

Becky Beaton, "VERACITY", Gibsons, B.C.

Paul Deyong's "Symbolic" a Taiwan Fisherman (Recipe p. 148).

MICROWAVES

MICROWAVE

MICROWAVES

Cooking techniques have advanced more in the past 25 years with the advent of microwave cooking than they did in the previous 250,000. Microwaves cook in a way never before possible, both physically and in time.

When I first heard of this marvelous appliance which could cook a strip of bacon in a minute, a potato in 4 minutes and 4-lb roast in 30, I was skeptical. When Capt. Vancouver ordered plum pudding for all aboard the "Discovery" on January 1, 1792, little did he know that one day the six-hour steaming process could be done in 15 minutes by a thing called a micro-wave.

This is not the time or place to learn to use your microwave so the following are just a few reminders on technique and tips for the galley.

UP ON MICROWAVES

TIME AND POWER

Although recipes are timed for a 600 watt oven, you will find in your travels that the voltage varies from marina to marina so that there could be a 10-20% variation in your microwave.

To adjust for this variable, check foods before they should be done — they can always be cooked a little more, if required. The microwave oven excels in cooking small portions but fear not the cooking of a beef roast. A boneless 3-4 lb rolled rib or sirloin tip roasts well in a microwave oven set on low (say 30-50%) using the lower power for less tender cuts. At 30%, cooking time to medium-rare would be 18 minutes per pound; at 50%, 12 minutes per pound.

A quick review on roasting would follow these lines:
— marinate tougher cuts (bbq section)
— don't salt before cooking
— set on rack to keep out of juices (drain occasionally)
— cover with wax paper
— turn over half way through cooking
— remove from oven before reaching desired temperature and let set covered for 10-15 minutes before carving (meat temperature will rise 10-15 degrees).

DEFROSTING

Leave chicken, steak, roasts, etc., in original package and place in paper bag. This will help prevent projecting parts from cooking. Defrost in cycles with rest periods in between.

REHEATING FOODS

Leftovers are best heated in a microwave oven as food doesn't dry out as it would in a conventional oven. Casseroles and stews are often better the next day when flavours have had a chance to blend. Reheat covered.

HOT TIPS

Use your microwave to:

— soften cream cheese or butter

— dry fresh breadcrumbs

— recrisp stale cereals, biscuits, chips

— heat individual servings of hot drinks

— warm citrus fruits in order to obtain more juice

— soften too hard ice cream

— heat brandy for your flambe

— Freshen or thaw breads, rolls, cakes — microwave in brown bag and serve as fresh.

HINTS FOR COOKING EGGS IN THE MICROWAVE

— Use the freshest possible

— Poach in barely simmering water — cover eggs at least 2 inches deep

— The longer they stay in water, the more they will cook

— A popping sound usually indicates over cooking

— For egg dishes use low or medium power settings to avoid overcooking

— Gently pierce yolk 2 to 3 times with a tooth pick to puncture membrane only.

MICROWAVE EGGWICH   SERVES 1

2 slices	toast buttered
1	egg
	salt and pepper
	ketchup (opt.)

Place one slice on paper towel on a plate. Break egg on toast. Season. Spread ketchup on 2nd piece (if desired). Lightly press on top of egg. Microwave full power $1^1/_4$ — $1^3/_4$ mins. Turn to prevent sogginess. Let stand 2 mins. (egg gets very hot)

EGGS & VEGIES

	1 egg	2 egg	4 egg	(600 w)
POACHED				
Boiling water	$^1/_4$ c	$^1/_2$ c	1 c	Boil water in dish. Break in eggs, pierce yolks.
Time in mins.	$^3/_4$	1	$2^1/_4$	Cover with plastic wrap.
SCRAMBLED				
Butter/marg.	1 t	2 t	4 t	Full power melt butter
Milk/water	1 t	2 t	4 t	mix all ingredients. Cover with plastic wrap, stir twice while cooking. Finish by standing 3 mins.
Time in mins.	1	$1^1/_2$	$2^1/_2$	(covered).

GREEN BEANS ITALIANO   SERVES 4

14 oz		Drain beans, reserving 2 T of liquid.
can	green beans	Combine all ingredients together
$^1/_2$ can	garbanzo beans	with reserved bean liquid,
2 T	pimiento	microwave on high till heated
2 T	black olives, sliced	through.
1	pepperoni, sliced	
2 T	olive oil	
1 clove	garlic, chopped	
$^1/_2$ t	oregano	

BAKED POTATOES

Place potatoes on paper towels and cook till slightly firm. Wrap tightly in foil for 5 mins. or till served. To crisp skin place in conventional oven at 350 degrees for 10 mins. Remove small potatoes from microwave early or put them in centre. Timing: 1 potato $3^1/_2$ — 4 mins.; 2 potatoes $6^1/_2$ — 7 mins.; 3 potatoes $8^1/_2$ — 9 mins.; 4 potatoes $10^1/_2$ — 11 mins.

MAURINE'S DO AHEAD MAGIC

POTATOES — Microwave in their skins wrapped individually with paper towels. On board potatoes can be quartered, peeled, sliced, used for main meal, breakfast or potato salad.

ROAST BEEF — Cook beef to taste, slice and put back together wrapped in foil. Make gravy at home. When finishing on board place a small amount of water in pan and heat beef in its foil wrapping in water covered until hot. Gravy or "au jus" may either be warmed or taken in a thermos. Serve on a bun with tossed salad. Leftover beef can be used for sandwiches or chopped and added to vegie soup mix.

HAM — As above — serve with Waldorf salad. Leftover ham can be saved for breakfast and/or added chopped in a packaged pea soup for lunch.

BACON — Microwave bacon at home until just undercooked. Drain on paper towel. Wrap in clean paper towel then in foil. Just needs heating before serving. This eliminates excess "grease" when cooking the limited space of the galley.

HAMBURGER (Ground Beef) — Cook at home, drain and package in ziplock bags and freeze for use in casseroles, chilies, spaghetti sauce, etc. Cook your patties and meat balls ahead and freeze also.
SO SAYS —

Maurine Paetkau, "MAURINE LADY", Abbotsford, B.C.

(MEN) When they are cooking . . . they won't let anyone near them. But if a woman is preparing a meal, try to keep them out of the kitchen.

LUCILLE BALL

SALMON WITH WINE   SERVES 4

1/4 c	dry white wine
2 T	butter
1 t	Dijon mustard or grated lemon peel
1/2 t	dillweed or tarragon
pinch	white pepper

Combine all ingredients in a dish just large enough for fish. Whisk together till blended.

4 —	
6 oz	salmon steaks

Arrange in dish, turning to coat, cover with plastic wrap. Microwave on high 6 mins. per lb. Let stand 2 mins. Spoon sauce over.

FILLETS & RICE   SERVES 4

1 1/2 c	quick cooking rice
1 1/2 c	chicken bouillon
2	gr. onions, sliced
1/2 t	curry powder
1 lb	fish fillets
2 T	lemon juice
1 T	butter

Stir rice, bouillon, onions and curry together in a 10 inch dish. Place fish on top, squeeze lemon juice over, dot with butter and cover with plastic wrap. Microwave on high 8 mins., let stand 6 mins.

LEMON-BUTTER SNAPPER   SERVES 4

1/4 c	butter
2 T	lemon juice
1 t	grated lemon peel
1/4 t	black pepper

Combine all ingredients in a 9″ round dish. Microwave on high 1 min. Stir together.

1 lb	fish fillets, split if thick

Arrange in dish, turning to coat, cover with plastic wrap. Microwave on high 6 mins., let stand 3 mins., spoon sauce over.

Paul Deyong, "SYMBOLIC", Vancouver, B.C.

The curious thing about fishing is you never want to go home. If you catch something, you can't stop. If you don't catch anything, you hate to leave in case something might bite.

CHICKEN CORDON BLEU

3	chicken breasts, boned, halved and skinned	Place between two pieces of wax paper and pound lightly to $^1/_4$ inch thickness.
6 slices 6 slices	ham Swiss cheese	Top each chicken piece with a slice of ham and cheese, roll and secure with toothpicks.
$^1/_2$ c $^1/_4$ c	corn flake crumbs parmesan cheese	Mix together to make seasoned crumbs.

Roll chicken pieces in seasoned crumbs, place on roasting rack, seam side down. Cover loosely with waxed paper. Microwave on medium power for five mins., rotate dish half a turn, cook on medium for 11 mins. longer or till chicken is tender and tops crisp.

Lloyd Bray, "PRISTINE", West Vancouver, B.C.

BROCCOLI CASSEROLE

$^1/_2$ c 2 T	onion, chopped butter	Cook on full power till tender.
2 T $^1/_2$ c 3 8 oz 1 lb to taste	flour water eggs, beaten med Cheddar cheese broccoli, cooked salt and pepper	Stir in flour, then water, then eggs, then grated cheese, lastly broccoli. Lay in 2″ deep dish.
	cornflake crumbs	Sprinkle with crumbs then cook 30–35 mins on defrost till knife comes out clean in centre. Garnish with tomato slices. Serve hot or cold.

Grace Maberg, "AMAZING GRACE", Halfmoon Bay, B.C.

SCALLOPED OYSTERS

SERVES 4-6

$3/4$ c	seasoned bread crumbs	Combine, spread $1/3$ of mixture in
$1/3$ c	melted butter	2 qt glass casserole.
1 pt	fresh oysters, drained	Reserve $1/2$ c oyster liquor. Layer
$1/2$ c	cream or milk	oysters over crumbs, combine
$1/3$ c	celery, diced	remaining ingredients except parsley
$1/2$ t ea.	Worcester sauce and salt	with reserved liquor and pour over oysters. Top with remaining crumbs
$1/4$ t	pepper	and parsley. Microwave on high 5
2 T	parsley, minced	mins., rotate $1/4$ turn, cook further 5 mins. Rest 5 mins. before serving.

Joyce Smethurst, "OBELIX", Gibsons, B.C.

THE PORK CHOP "PHOTO-FINISH"

SERVES 4

4	pork chops $1/2''$ thick	Defrost beans enough to separate and pile around chops in an $8'' \times 8''$
10 oz pkg	frozen green beans	dish.
2 T	butter	Melt butter, add flour to make paste,
2 T	flour	gradually add milk stirring
$1^1/2$ c	milk	constantly. Add rest of ingredients,
$1/4$ c	prepared horseradish	microwave high 3 mins. stirring
$1/4$ t ea.	salt and pepper	every minute. Pour over chops and beans.
$1/2$ c	bread or cornflake crumbs	Sprinkle on top, microwave high 6 mins., rotate $1/4$ turn, cook further 6 mins.
$1/4$ c	parmesan cheese	Sprinkle on top, microwave 3 mins. Rest 5 mins.

Moira Clement, "SPORTSPAL", Gibsons, B.C.

This "Photo-Finish" was really a day late!!

MICROWAVE SAUCES

HOLLANDAISE

¹/₄ c	butter	Microwave butter in 1 c glass
3 T	lemon juice	measure on med/high 1 min. to
3	egg yolks	melt. Beat in lemon juice then egg
¹/₄ t	salt	yolks then salt till smooth.

Microwave med/high 1 min. stirring every 15 secs. Cook 15 secs. longer for thicker sauce.

CHEDDAR CHEESE

2 T	butter	Microwave butter in 4 c glass
2 T	A/p flour	measure on high 1 min. Blend in
1 c	milk	flour, microwave high 30 secs.
¹/₄ t	dry mustard	Whisk in milk and seasonings. Cook
to taste	salt and bl. pepper	high 2 mins., whisk, cook 2 mins.
³/₄ c	Cheddar cheese, grated	more till thick. Stir in cheese.

BARBEQUE SAUCE

2 T	vegetable oil	Place oil and garlic in 4 c glass
2 cloves	garlic, chopped	measure. Microwave high 2 mins.
2 T	brown sugar	Stir in remaining ingredients.
¹/₂ c	ketchup	Microwave high 2 mins. Stir.
¹/₄ c	chicken broth or water	Microwave 3 more mins.
1 T	dried mustard	
1 T	Worcester sauce	

CARAMEL CREAM

²/₃ c	brown sugar	Measure sugar, butter, cream and
¹/₄ c	unsalted butter	syrup into 4 c glass measure, cover
¹/₄ c	half and half cream	loosely with plastic wrap, microwave
2 T	corn syrup	high 2 mins., stir, microwave 2 more mins.

¹/₂ t	vanilla extract	Stir in. Serve over ice cream.

Gypsy V at Anchor Seymour Inlet '87. By Author. (Recipes 46, 77, 81).

D
E
S
S
E
R
T
S

Marie Antoinette had not yet declared, "Let them eat cake", and it may be true, when Capt. George sailed the gulf, that neither he nor his crew had the finale to their evening meal of "Strawberries Alborozadas" or "Mocha Cream-filled Profiteroles". What they did have, however, was wattleberries and strawberries, gathered while at a Gulf Island anchorage. Quote Vancouver's log, " . . . Mr. Broughton found a great quantity of very excellent strawberries which gave it (the bay) the name 'Strawberry Bay' (48°, 34'N; 122°, 43'W).

STRAWBERRIES ALBOROZADAS

2-15 oz cans	strawberries	Drain strawberries, set aside. Add water to reserved juice to make
1/2 c	sugar	1 1/2 cups, simmer with sugar and
2 T	lemon peel, grated	lemon peel for 10 mins.
2 T	water	Combine, add to above, simmer
1 T	cornstarch	stirring until thickened.
1/3 c	tequila	Warm.
1 pt	strawberry ice cream chocolate shavings, semi-sweet strips of lemon peel	Scoop ice cream into serving dishes, top with reserved strawberries. Top strawberry sauce with tequila and ignite while pouring over ice cream. Garnish with chocolate and peel. STAND BACK WHEN IGNITING SPIRITS.

Art McGinnis, "GIBSONS MARINA", Gibsons, B.C.

CHOCOLATE MACAROONS

1¹/₂ c	sugar	Combine in saucepan and bring to boil.
¹/₂ c	shortening or marg.	
¹/₂ c	milk	
5 T	cocoa	Add and stir briskly.
3 c	quick cooking oats	Add, stirring constantly.
1 c	coconut	
1 t	vanilla	Add and stir well. Drop by the tablespoon onto wax paper and cool overnight.
¹/₄ t	salt	

Doreen Avery, "TWINKLETOES", Gibsons, B.C.

IMPOSSIBLE COCONUT PIE

4	eggs	Beat.
2 c	milk	Add and stir.
³/₄ c	sugar	
¹/₂ c	butter, melted	
2 T	vanilla	
pinch	salt	
¹/₂ c	flour	Add, pour into greased 10″ pie plate.
1 c	coconut	Sprinkle on top then bake in 350 degree oven for 1 hr.

Jim McKay, "COLLEEN", Vancouer, B.C.

PILGRIM PUMPKIN PIE

1²/₃ c	evaporated milk
1¹/₂ c	canned pumpkin
1 c	sugar
2	eggs, well beaten
1 t	salt
¹/₂ t ea.	cinnamon, ginger, allspice, nutmeg and cloves

Blend all ingredients together thoroughly. Pour into unbaked pie shell, bake 15 mins. at 450 degrees, then 35 mins. at 350 degrees.

The cutter "CRESSET" was designed and built in 1929 by the Uri brothers who designed the Burrard St. bridge (picture page   ). She was built of local lumber on the site of the Vancouver Aquatic Centre. After winning the first Swiftsure Race she became renowned as a fast boat. She has been sailing the coast for 60 years and is presently moored at the Vancouver Rowing Club.

Jan Mayall, "CRESSET", Vancouver, B.C.

PEANUT PIE

SERVES 8 +

20	Ritz crackers
1 c	peanuts, salted and roasted
1 c	sugar

Finely crush the crackers and peanuts, combine with sugar.

3	egg whites
¹/₄ t	cream of tartar
	whipped cream

Beat till stiff, adding cream of tartar while beating, fold into above. Can be made in pie plate or square for bars. Top with whipped cream after baking if desired.

Julie Jones, "AURORA", Los Angeles, Ca.

Discussion is an exchange of knowledge; argument an exchange of ignorance.

ROBERT QUILLEN

BRANDIED PEACHES

28 oz can	peach halves	Drain and place in shallow pan.
2 T	syrup from peaches	Combine and pour over peaches,
4 T	butter, melted	bake at 350 degrees for 25 mins.,
$^1/_2$ c	brown sugar	basting occasionally.
$^1/_4$ c	brandy	
$^1/_4$ t	cinnamon	

Jean Ambrose, "M/V CHANGI", W. Vancouver, B.C.

PEARS AU CHOCOLAT   SERVES 4

2-15 oz cans	pear halves, drained	Arrange in shallow pan and set aside.
$^1/_3$ c	fresh orange juice	Combine ingredients and simmer for
$^1/_4$ c	brown sugar, firmly packed	10 mins. Pour over pears and cool.
$^1/_4$ c	water	
1 t	orange rind, grated	
4-serving size	Jello chocolate pudding mix	To create sauce, combine mix, sugar and water, heat over med. heat till
1 c	water	bubbling, stir in butter. Add brandy if
$^1/_2$ c	sugar	needed to make sauce pourable.
2 T	butter or marg.	Serve over pears.
1 T	brandy (pt.)	

Ruth McGinnis, "GIBSONS MARINA", Gibsons, B.C.

It is when you are safe at home that you wish you were having an adventure. When you are having an adventure you wish you were safe at home.

THORNTON WILDER

EASY CHOCOLATE CAKE

3 c	flour	Combine all ingredients. Make a well
2 c	sugar	in centre.
8 T	cocoa	
4 t	baking powder	
2 t	baking soda	
1¹/₂ t	salt	

3	eggs, beaten	Add enough water to eggs to total
2 T	vinegar	2 c. Add to other ingredients, pour
10 T	vegetable oil	into well, beat with electric mixer at
2 t	vanilla	med speed for 2 mins. Pour into
		9″ × 13″ pan and bake 50 mins. at
		350 degrees.

Cool and ice as desired or TRY THIS —

8 oz		Blend together.
pkg	soft cream cheese	
¹/₄ c	sugar	

1 pt	whipping cream	Beat till stiff and fold in.

Slice cake into two layers. Spread 1st layer with cherry pie filling, place 2nd layer on top and spread and ice with above mixture. Garnish with maraschino cherries and shaved chocolate. (Add a touch of your favourite liqueur to pie filling).

Dot Gibson, "MALIS", Tofino, B.C.

RUM BALLS BACARDI

MAKES 2¹/₂ DOZEN

50	vanilla wafers	Crumble wafers and combine with
¹/₄ c	Bacardi amber rum	other ingredients. Roll into 1″ balls.
¹/₄ c	honey	
1 c	ground walnuts	

	icing sugar	Roll balls in sugar.

Donald Mosedale, "PINOCCHIO", W. Vancouver, B.C.

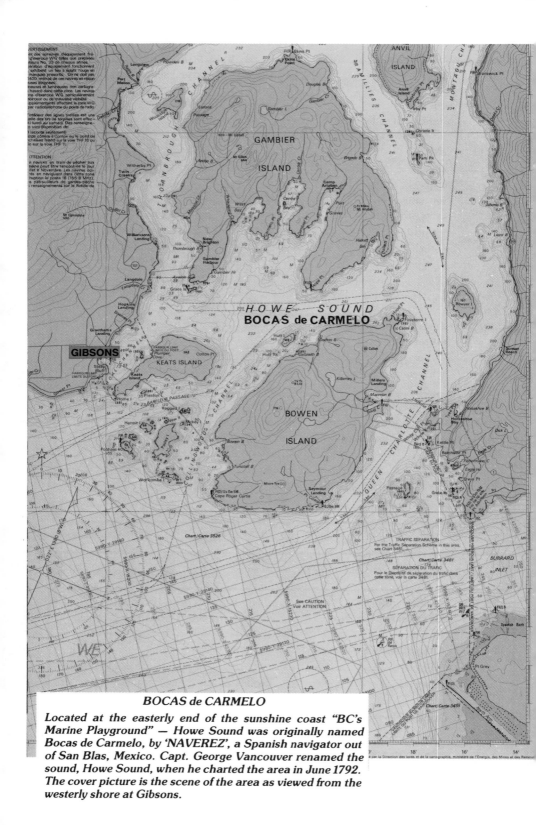

BOCAS de CARMELO

*Located at the easterly end of the sunshine coast "BC's
Marine Playground" — Howe Sound was originally named
Bocas de Carmelo, by 'NAVEREZ', a Spanish navigator out
of San Blas, Mexico. Capt. George Vancouver renamed the
sound, Howe Sound, when he charted the area in June 1792.
The cover picture is the scene of the area as viewed from the
westerly shore at Gibsons.*

PUNCHES

FROSTY FRUIT COOLERS

HOT SPIRITED DRINKS

DRINKS

In June of 1792 Captain George Vancouver set the Discovery's anchor on the northwest coast of North America in a small anchorage known as Birch Bay. While on a 12-day excursion exploring Bocas de Carmelo, the Sunshine Coast and Jervis Inlet on B.C.'s west coast, Vancouver's brewmaster went ashore to make spruce beer using ingredients from the spruce tree. This contributed to the safe return home of all of the ship's crew, free from the scourge of scurvy.

From Alaska to Mexico, let's toast, "Capt. George Vancouver".

"Then a smile, and a glass, and a toast and a cheer for all the good wine, and we've got some of it here!"

Oliver Wendell Holmes

PUNCHES

Some recipes call for marinating fruits (when present) for a day or two. Happily this is not the case for these west cost varieties — an hour is acceptable to combine strong and weak or tart and sweet flavours. The following punches are designed to serve 8 to 10 or so.

ALASKAN GLACIAL BLUE

| 12 oz | Blue Curacao | Chill ingredients thoroughly and stir well. |
| 4 oz | lemon juice | |

| 48 oz | dry champagne | Add and stir gently. |

Cut peel of two lemons into strips, say $2'' \times \frac{1}{4}''$, and float on top, yellow side up.

B.C. CELEBRATION

28 oz		Chop peaches lightly. Stir with juice and other ingredients.
tin	peaches	
2 c	sugar	
1 c	lemon juice	
4 c	ice water	
24 oz	dry white wine	

| 48 oz | dry champagne | Stir gently. |

| 4 c | strawberries | Use fresh or frozen as garnish. |

WASHINGTON SALUTE

40 oz	cranberry juice	Chill all ingredients and mix well. Serve over ice.
24 oz	dry white wine	
16 oz	club soda	

| | fresh fruit chunks | Garnish |

OREGONIAN CHAMPAGNE ROSE

$^1/_2$	lemon rind shredded	Stir to dissolve sugar.
4 T	sugar	
2 T	lemon juice	
24 oz	dry red wine	Add and stir.
48 oz	champagne	Add and stir gently. Serve over ice.
48 oz	club soda	
	fruit of season	Garnish.

CALIFORNIA BREEZE *(Assemble ice ring the day before)*

6 c	water	Half fill ring mold and freeze.
	lemon slices	Remove mold from freezer. Arrange
	peach halves	fruit in pattern. Top with water and
	strawberries	refreeze. Tip in hot water to remove ring.
24 oz	dry white wine	Assemble chilled ingredients in
48 oz	club soda	punch bowl.
4 oz	brandy	
3 oz	creme de menthe	
2 doz	strawberries	
24 oz	champagne	Add just before serving, stir gently and slide in ice ring.

MEXICAN FIESTA

5 oz can	frozen lemon concentrate	Using undiluted juices, mix together and chill. Just before serving pour over ice.
5 oz can	frozen grapefruit concentrate	
14 oz can	fruit cocktail, drained	
24 oz	Bacardi white rum	
36 oz	club soda, chilled	Stir in gently.

FROSTY FRUIT COOLERS

Bright, colourful fruit juices combined with soda water and poured over ice make ideal summer drinks. Served with or without a splash of gin, vodka or rum, they are "coolers". If you do not have a blender on board, use prepared juices.

WATERMELON SPRITZER   *SERVES 4*

3 lb	watermelon	Remove seeds and rind from
8	thin slices ginger	watermelon, chop pulp reserving
1 t	lemon juice	some for garnish. Combine in
$^1/_4$ t	salt	blender, puree and strain.

6 oz	club soda	Add, stir and garnish with watermelon chunks.

MINTED CANTALOUPE SPRITZER   *SERVES 4*

1	ripe cantaloupe	Remove seeds and rind from
$^1/_2$ c	fresh mint	cantaloupe and chop pulp finely. Combine in blender, puree and strain.

$^1/_4$ c	yogurt	Add and blend.

6 oz	club soda	Mix and serve over ice. Garnish with mint sprig.

ORANGE-BEET SPRITZER   *SERVES 4*

1 med	beet	Peel and dice.

	zest of 1 orange	Combine with beet in blender and
$1^1/_2$ c	orange juice	puree till smooth.

8 oz	club soda	Add and stir. Garnish with orange
$1^1/_2$ c	orange juice	juice.

HOT SPIRITED DRINKS

Nothing so fortifies warm friendships on a bleak afternoon (that November day in July) or makes cozy gatherings cozier than a "cup" of something strong and steaming. Remember that alcohol vaporizes at 172 F so don't overheat your hot spirited drinks — do, however, serve them in suitably warm heavy mugs or glasses. Place a spoon in your glasses when adding hot liquid to avoid breakage.

HOT SHERRY EGGNOG   SERVES 4

1¹/₂ c	milk	Scald in double boiler.
2 T	sugar	Beat together, then stir in a little milk
2	egg yolks	— return to double boiler and cook.
pinch	nutmeg, cinnamon	
5 oz	sherry	Stir in slowly and serve hot.

HOT CRANBERRY TODDY   SERVES 4

4 oz	brandy	Divide equally among 4 mugs.
3 c	cranberry cocktail	Heat but don't boil. Pour into mugs
1 t	orange zest	with cinnamon sticks.

HOT SCOT   SERVES 4

¹/₂ c	Scotch whiskey	Divide equally among 4 mugs or
¹/₄ c	Drambuie	glasses.
1 t	bitters	
1 qt	milk	Heat but don't boil, strain into mugs
4 T	butter	and add butter.

A soft drink turneth away company.

OLIVER HERFORD

A LOG OF SHIPS

SEE ALSO COMPLETE INDEXES AT BEGINNING OF EACH CHAPTER

Gibsons Marina at dawn.
SYD SPAAN PHOTO

SEND ME a 6-PAK • GALLEY MAGIC

At $65.00 Postage Paid (Can.)

At $48.00 Postage Paid (US)

☐ Payment Encl.   ☐ VISA   ☐ Mastercard   ☐ Amex

NAME _____

ADDRESS _____   CARD # _____

CITY _____ PROV. (STATE) _____   EXPIRY _____

POSTAL CODE (ZIP) _____

Signature

Shipped on Receipt of Order — Prices Subject to Change

SEND MY FRIEND • GALLEY MAGIC

A copy or _____ copies.
At $12.95 plus $1.55 postage and handling per book. (Can.)
Or $9.75 plus $1.25 postage and handling per book (U.S.)
$0.50 Gift Wrap

HIS NAME IS _____   MESSAGE

ADDRESS _____

CITY _____ PROV (STATE) _____

POSTAL CODE (ZIP) _____

BILL ME _____   CARD # _____

ADDRESS _____

CITY _____ PROV (STATE) _____   EXPIRY _____

POSTAL (ZIP) _____

Signature

☐ Payment Encl.   ☐ VISA   ☐ Mastercard   ☐ Amex

Shipped On Receipt Of Order — Prices Subject to Change

SEND ME • GALLEY MAGIC

Please send me _____ copies of Galley Magic at $12.95 plus $1.55 postage
and handling per book. (Can.)

Or $9.75 plus $1.25 postage and handling per book (U.S.)

☐ Payment Encl.   ☐ VISA   ☐ Mastercard   ☐ Amex

NAME _____

ADDRESS _____   CARD # _____

CITY _____ PROV. (STATE) _____   EXPIRY _____

POSTAL CODE (ZIP) _____

Signature

Shipped on Receipt of Order — Prices Subject to Change

TO ORDER: "GALLEY MAGIC"

Fill in reverse and mail with payment details to:

> Bocas de Carmelo Publishing
> c/o Gibsons Marina
> Box 1520
> Gibsons, B.C. V0N 1V0

TO ORDER: "GALLEY MAGIC"

Fill in reverse and mail with payment details to:

> Bocas de Carmelo Publishing
> c/o Gibsons Marina
> Box 1520
> Gibsons, B.C. V0N 1V0

All copies will be sent to same address unless otherwise specified. If you wish one or any number of books sent as gifts, furnish a list of names and addresses of recipients. If you wish to enclose your own gift card with each book, please write name of recipient on outside of the envelope, enclose with order, and we will include it with your gift.

TO ORDER: "GALLEY MAGIC"

Fill in reverse and mail with payment details to:

> Bocas de Carmelo Publishing
> c/o Gibsons Marina
> Box 1520
> Gibsons, B.C. V0N 1V0